Orientation for Leaders

A Manual for Training Church Leaders

Richard B. Ramsay

Orientation for Leaders

A Manual for Training
Church Leaders

Richard B. Ramsay

ISBN: **979-8-90148-582-8**
Staten House

(The 2025 edition is formated with slightly larger pages and
has a new ISBN number. Otherwise, the content is the same
as the 2019 edition.)

Contents

The Author

Dr. Ramsay was a missionary in Chile for 21 years, teaching in a seminary and planting churches. There he met his wife, Angelica. They now live in Florida. They have two children, both married. For the past 25 years, they have worked internationally in distance education, traveling to teach classes and producing resources for theological education and leadership training. Richard has taught for *Universidad FLET* and *Thirdmill Seminary* and has developed many online courses.

He holds a D.Min. degree and an M.Div. from *Westminster Theological Seminary*, as well as a Th.M. from *Covenant Theological Seminary.*

Other books by the author include *The Certainty of the Faith, Am I Good Enough?, Basic Greek and Exegesis, Intellectual Integrity, Catholics and Protestants, Transformed into the Image of Jesus, Synopsis of the Bible,* and *Putting the Pieces Together.*

Preface

As Steve Brown says, if you can't stand problems, you should stay away from the Church! He admits that the Church has many flaws, but he still loves her. Above all, he loves the Church because Christ loves her. In fact, Christ loves the Church so much that He gave His life for her, and will purify her until she is glorious and without blemish (Ephesians 5:25-27).[1]

The Bible says that the task of pastors and teachers is to train the members of their church to minister to others, and that the goal of the Church is that we all become like Christ. This means that we are all "ministers" and that we can all participate in working toward this amazing goal. To stay away is not an option.

> And he gave the apostles, the prophets, the evangelists, the shepherds and teachers, to equip the saints for the work of ministry, for building up the body of Christ, until we all attain to the unity of the faith and of the knowledge of the Son of God, to mature manhood, to the measure of the stature of the fullness of Christ. (Ephesians 4:11-13)

The purpose of this book is to help accomplish our noble task. Some of these lessons were originally prepared to help train leaders in Chile. For 21 years, I served there as a missionary, teaching at a seminary and planting churches. As we started new churches, we saw the need for Bible study materials for training new leaders, not only to solidify their

---

[1] Steve Brown, "Big on Church," Key Life, <https://www.keylife.org/articles/big-on-church>, May 31, 2017.

biblical and theological knowledge, which is absolutely essential, but also to help them develop the skills for practical aspects of the ministry, and to help them grow spiritually.

For the past 20 years, my wife Angelica and I have been living in Miami, working in distance education. We prepare resources and travel to teach in different countries. In the context of this ministry, people have asked me about resources for training leaders. This manual is a combination of the first materials used in Chile and other materials used in more recent years, especially in Cuba, Spain, and Central America.

The book is meant for all kinds of "ministers." It is especially for the training of elders and deacons. It might even be helpful as a brief initial practical orientation for pastors. But it is also appropriate for anyone who wants to serve in the church, whether they are lay people or officers, men or women, adults or young people.

I recommend studying the book, section by section, answering the questions written in *italics*, then answering the review questions and reflection questions in the shaded areas. Some sections also include practical exercises to be completed. Ideally, the reader would be part of a church study group. If so, you can review a chapter at each meeting, discussing the questions and sharing the results of the exercises. Some groups may prefer to skip a chapter, or to study the chapters in a different order. Feel free to use the book in the way it is most helpful for you and your group.

We also encourage you to form some kind of mentoring relationship with the pastor or some leader of your church. It might be the same person who is the facilitator of your study group. I recommend that you meet regularly with your mentor, to talk and pray, and to share how you are practicing some of the activities of the ministry studied in this book. The mentor can simply ask questions like the following: a) How are you doing?, b) How is your family doing?, c) What is the most meaningful thing you have been learning in your studies?, d) What have you been learning from your ministry experiences?, e) Is there anything I can help you with? and f) What would you like us to pray for? This will make sure that the preparation is not only academic.

Hopefully, the mentor will also invite you to come along side him in some of his activities, like visiting someone in the hospital or leading a Bible study, for example. Then it would be great if he could also accompany you in your ministry activities, and give you feedback. Our son is currently in his fourth year of medical school, and I have often thought that our seminaries and all leadership training should be more like medical school. Apparently they learned their methods from Jesus! The candidates study intensely, but they also follow experienced doctors around to observe, then the doctors begin to let them give their initial diagnosis and talk over particular cases, and in their final years, they practice their specialty under the careful observation of experienced doctors. The best way to learn is to follow the example of another person who has more experience in the ministry, and to discuss everything with that person, in the same way the disciples learned from Jesus.

Introduction; Lessons from My "Wonder Garden"

Reflections on the sovereignty of God and the responsibility of man

I always love to take care of the grass and the plants in our yard. But when we moved to a sector of Viña del Mar in Chile, it was a long difficult process to get them looking nice. Soon I began to notice that things were happening in the church in much the same way as they were happening in my garden. What was the Lord teaching me?!

First, there was little grass when we arrived, and the ground was dry. The same thing was true for the spiritual reality of our neighborhood: there was no evangelical church in the area where we lived, we didn't know anybody, and there seemed to be a resistance to the gospel.

In my yard, I had to start by working with the soil. I bought a truckload of topsoil, dug up the hard ground, mixed the better soil, smoothed it out, planted new seeds, then watered and watered. The grass grew and looked nice for a short time,... then it died. I realized that I had bought some pretty cheap topsoil the first time, and had to buy another truckload, of better quality this time. I started over, mixed the dirt, planted the seeds, and watered and watered. The grass grew and looked beautiful for a while,... then it died again. Finally, I talked to an expert about my lawn. He asked me if there was a lot of sun in my yard, or if there was a lot of shade. I told him there were many trees that produced a lot of shade, and he recommended a special seed for shade. I started all over again, and this time it worked!

In the church-planting project, our first efforts didn't bear much fruit either. We tried to get acquainted with neighbors, and we tried to break down barriers of resistance, but it seemed to be in vain. Few people in that area would go to a worship service of a new Protestant church. We had to prepare the soil and find better ways to reach people. We didn't need a new message; the gospel is the same. But we needed to learn how to communicate it in ways that were more appropriate for our context. For us, this meant starting English classes to meet people. Then we began to hold conferences, have informal men's breakfasts in a hotel restaurant, invite women to teas in a similar neutral environment, and we had workshops on marriage and family. Finally, one contact led to another, and the church began to grow!

Another lesson I learned from the garden was that some plants around the edge near the wall seemed to be dead, but they were actually still alive. Sometimes I would tell my wife, Angelica, that I was going to dig up a plant and throw it away, but she would always encourage me to wait a little longer. The same thing happened in the church: sometimes we thought someone had totally lost interest, then they came back.

Unfortunately, sometimes just the opposite happened. In the garden, some plants looked strong for a while, then they died. In the church there were also people who appeared to be touched by the gospel, then later fell away. During several months we did a Bible study with a neighbor lady once a week. At the end of the study, as we did the last chapter of the book, I felt it was time to ask if she wanted to make a decision. I thought she had understood the gospel and was ready to turn her life over to Christ. But after a heartfelt invitation, she just stared at me, stone cold and indifferent!

Introduction

The most important lesson I learned from the garden was that some beautiful plants were growing nicely, even though I had not planted them! I don't know if the wind blew the seeds over from another garden, or maybe they had been buried for a while without growing. I really don't have a good scientific explanation. That's why I like to call it my "wonder garden." To me, these were miracles. In the church, something similar happened: people that nobody knew just showed up! One Sunday, a new family arrived, and the missionaries began to talk among ourselves about who had invited them. But nobody had invited them! After the service, the father told me that he had met a Pentecostal pastor on a trip, and that the conversation had stirred his interest in spiritual things. He knew that his sister attended a church in Santiago, so he called her to ask if she knew of any church in Viña del Mar. His sister had a copy of one of my discipleship books, and it had the name of our church on the back. No address, just the name and the city. So the man called the police to ask if they knew about our church, and they told him about the house where we had our services!

This whole experience helped me to understand a little better how God's sovereignty relates to human responsibility. We can't sit passively with our arms crossed, waiting for God to bless. If we don't work on the soil, plant seeds, and water them, we can't expect the garden to be beautiful. However, we can't control the results either. We don't control the height of the plants, the shape of the leaves, the color of the flowers, or the beauty of the garden. And thankfully, God sometimes does surprising, miraculous things! That's the way it works in the ministry, in fact that's the way it works in all of life. Living by faith means doing what God asks of us, and leaving the results in His hands. I believe we should keep this fundamental principle in mind for all matters relating to church ministry.

Read 1 CORINTHIANS 3:6.

What did Paul and Apollos do?

Who caused the growth?

REVIEW QUESTIONS

1. Explain the author's experience of planting a garden and planting a church at the same time. In general, what happened?

2. What lessons did he learn from this experience? What is his main conclusion?

REFLECTION QUESTIONS

1. Have you ever had an experience similar to the author's garden experience. Have you had any experience in the ministry similar to his?

2. How would you apply these lessons from the garden to other areas of life, such as raising a family or managing a business?

Chapter 1: Our Church; Its Identity and Ministry

What ...right has the Church to exist anyway?
Is religion simply the hokum that supports
the comedians of the pulpit?

Sinclair Lewis[2]

How could we respond to Sinclair Lewis?

While people often consider the Church our spiritual "mother," far too many would also add that she has been a rather bad mother. In this chapter, we will explore the biblical concept of the identity and ministry of the Church. I hope it will encourage you to love the Church more, even with its failures and imperfections.

Our study will make it clear that the Church not only has a "right" to exist, but that it has been established by God Himself with an important purpose in this world. While there may be "comedians" in some pulpits who are seeking their own benefit, I would not consider them representatives of the true Church. God intends something very different for His Church. But first, let's look at some erroneous views.

We need to distinguish between the Church in the universal sense and the church as a local congregation. I will be speaking especially of the Church in its universal sense in

---

[2] Sinclair Lewis, quoted by Richard Lingeman in *Sinclair Lewis; Rebel from Main Street* (St. Paul MN: Borealis Books, 2002), 275.

this chapter, as we define its identity and ministry, but at the end of the chapter we will see how this affects the local church.[3]

1.1. What is the Church?

a. Erroneous Views of the Church

The Church is weak and insignificant.

When I was in college, every day as I walked to class, I saw students on campus carrying signs, protesting against racism, war, and other social problems. I admired them, because they were willing to fight for a cause. Then on Sundays, in church, although we talked about important things related to the Bible and theology, I don't remember much conversation about social problems. For a time, I thought the church was not going to change the world. Only when I was in seminary did I learn that the Church was established by God, and that it was a fundamental instrument for solving the problems of humanity.

I then decided that if the Church was not fulfilling its mission properly, I should help it, rather than abandon it or just criticize it. I also realized that the changes we want to see in the world cannot be produced only by protests or by making new laws. The first change that has to happen is a change in the heart of man. The spiritual transformation

---

[3] We will use a capital "C" in this book when we speak of the Church in the universal sense and a small "c" when we speak of the local church.

comes first, then other changes are possible. Therefore, evangelism, teaching and discipleship have a priority in the ministry of the Church. I did not lose my conviction that we should fight against injustice, poverty, racism, and war, or that we should try to improve every aspect of society. However, I gained new hope about the key role that the Church can play in the process, and I changed my focus about how to achieve those changes.

In his book, *Haven of the Masses*, Christian Lalive D'Epinay analyzes Pentecostalism in Chile. He suggests that evangelicals in Chile have used the church as a refuge from the world, and that they are not involved in changing society. Instead, they have formed an isolated subculture in their church, where they feel more secure.[4]

I won't deny that some evangelicals take inappropriate refuge in their local churches, avoiding contact with the world. But I think the criticism is exaggerated, and I think Pentecostals and other evangelicals in Chile have changed a lot since 1969, when d'Epinay published his book. They do a lot to help those in need, including soup kitchens for the poor and programs for drug addicts, alcoholics, the elderly, and people with physical disabilities. When the Chilean parliament discussed legal rights for evangelicals, many politicians told stories of people who had received help from evangelicals and whose lives had been transformed. As a result, they decided to give them new privileges in 1999. The Church in Chile has not been so weak and impotent after all. The same thing can be said in many other countries.

---

[4] Christian Lalive d'Epinay, *Haven of the Masses; A Study of the Pentecostal Movement in Chile* (London: Lutterworth Press, 1969), 38.

The Church is a political instrument.

On the other extreme, some see the Church as a powerful instrument that transforms society through its political influence. The relationship between Church and State has often been a source of conflict. During the first few centuries after Christ, the Church was often persecuted. Then after Constantine (Edict of Milan in 313 AD), Christianity played a very dominant and influential role in Europe. At times, the Church seemed to have authority over the State, reflected in the moment when Pope Leo III crowned Charlemagne in 800, symbolizing his superiority.

Reformers began to realize the need to separate the spheres of authority in some way, but the change was gradual. John Calvin proposed that the State should govern "civil justice and outward morality," and that the Church should oversee the things of the "soul or inner man."[5] But they did not make a clear separation between the tasks of Church and State until two centuries after Calvin, when they modified the chapter on civil magistrates in the *Westminster Confession of Faith*.[6]

When the new countries were colonized in the Americas, freedom of religion was an essential issue. The countries with the largest Protestant populations were the first to establish a clear separation between Church and State. Early leaders in the United States spoke of a "wall of separation" (Thomas

---

[5] John Calvin, *Institutes of the Christian Religion,* ed. John T. McNeaill, trans. Ford Lewis Battles (Philadelphia: The Westminster Press, 1967), IV, 20, 1.

[6] Compare the 1647 version of the *Westminster Confession of Faith* with the 1788 version, chapter 23, paragraph III. < https://www.opc.org/documents/WCF_orig.html > (June 21, 2017).

Jefferson). The first amendment (1791) to the constitution forbids the establishment of an official religion and guarantees religious freedom.[7]

The countries of Latin America were slower to "un-establish" their official religion, which was Catholicism (Guatemala, 1871, México, 1874, Cuba 1902, Panamá, 1904, Uruguay, 1919, Chile, 1925, Paraguay, 1992). In Costa Rica, while the constitution of 1949 guarantees freedom of religion, it still leaves Catholicism as the official religion. In countries such as Argentina, the Dominican Republic, El Salvador, Honduras, and Peru, Catholicism has a special recognition in their constitution, but it is not a state religion.[8]

In recent years, we have seen renewed tendencies to consider the Church an instrument of political transformation. On the one hand, representatives of liberation theology have sought to use the Church to promote their revolutionary movement. On the other hand, some evangelicals also have used the platform of the Church to promote their conservative political agenda.

While the Church should always give biblical guidelines for ethical and social issues, I think it is dangerous when churches and church leaders identify themselves too closely with particular candidates or political parties. History shows that candidates and parties that may have seemed good at one time can have serious problems later, and it is difficult to change the image of having identified with them.

Furthermore, whereas in the Old Testament, the nation of Israel was the earthly representation of the kingdom of God,

---

[7] < https://constitution.congress.gov/constitution/amendment-1/ > (06/23/17)

[8] Wikipedia, «State Religion»: <http://en.wikipedia.org/wiki/State_religion> (6/15/ 2010), also «Costa Rica».

it is no longer represented by any one political nation, but by the Church. The kingdom of God spreads throughout different countries and different cultures. Just as Jesus always pointed to deeper issues and to longer-lasting changes, I believe the Church is called to influence in other more effective ways, without making the Church a political instrument that is tied to more temporary causes.

The Church exists for my personal happiness.

Some people think of the local church as a social club, where they meet friends, and where they can have fun. Once I talked to some young people who attended a youth meeting where they watched a secular movie and ate pizza, but nothing else. They commented later, "If we're only going to do that, we might as well stay home!" If the church doesn't offer spiritual care, what special contribution does it make? Also, I think we often underestimate the desire of young people to learn and study seriously. They want to be respected and treated like mature people. Of course this does not mean we should eliminate all fun or wholesome social activities that are appropriate for the church.

Others go to church with the purpose of seeking a solution to their economic and physical problems. The "prosperity" movement emphasizes these aspects in a disproportionate way. As we will analyze later, one of the areas of ministry of the Church is to help people with their physical and material needs. Furthermore, it is true that we have biblical promises that someday we will lack nothing, we will have no diseases, and there will be no tears (Revelation 21:1-4). However, this will not happen until Christ returns to establish the eternal form of His kingdom. Just as the first-century Jews didn't understand that the Messiah would come in different stages, some Christians today are also confused, thinking that we should *now* be experiencing *all* the benefits of the Kingdom of God. However, a closer reading of the Bible will teach us that while some promises have been fulfilled *already* (for example, we are forgiven and justified), others are *in process* (we are being sanctified), and others are *not yet* fulfilled at all (for example, we still do not have a new earth, renewed bodies, or total freedom from the physical and spiritual effects of the Fall).

Read ROMANS 8:14-30.

Write down some of the benefits of salvation that we ALREADY have when we believe in Christ. (Look for verbs in present tense, like "are", and other phrases such as "we have received.")

List some of the benefits of our salvation that we still do NOT YET experience until Christ returns. (Look at verbs in the future tense, and for concepts such as "waiting" for something.)

List some benefits that are IN PROCESS. (See especially verse 14 and verses 26-30.)

The Church does not exist primarily for our happiness, but for the glory of God. When Israel was delivered from slavery in Egypt, after crossing the Red Sea, the first thing they did was sing praises to the Lord (Exodus 15). In the same way,

21

the Church is the redeemed people of God, and its first priority is to gather to worship Him.

Read 1 CORINTHIANS 10:31.

What should be our motive for everything we do?

REVIEW QUESTIONS

1. Name and explain the erroneous views of the Church mentioned in this section. Make sure you include the view of the "prosperity" movement.

2. Explain why these views are wrong.

REFLECTION QUESTIONS

1. What do you think of the distorted perspectives of the Church mentioned in this section? Is there anything valid in them? What caused these views to arise? Make sure you include the view of the "prosperity" movement.

2. Can you think of other distorted views of the Church? What are they?

b. The Biblical View of the Church

What do we learn about the identity of the Church in the following passages? What figures are used?

EPHESIANS 1:22-23

1 CORINTHIANS 3.9

1 CORINTHIANS 3:16

1 PETER 2:5

1 PETER 2:9

JOHN 15:5

Pedro Arana says, "...We should consider the Church from a Trinitarian perspective, as the People of God, the Body of Christ, and the Community of the Holy Spirit."[9]

Greek and Hebrew Terms

In the Greek New Testament, one of the most common words for "church" is *ekklesía*.[10] The word "ecclesiastic" comes from the same root word. It means *assembly, congregation*, the *called*. It is a combination of two words:

ek is a preposition that means *out of, from, by,* or *away from*.

kaléo is a verb that means *to call*.

In the Hebrew Old Testament, the equivalent is *kajal*, meaning *convocation, congregation,* or *assembly*. In the

---

[9] Pedro Arana Quiroz, *Iniciación Cristiana* [Christian Initiation] (Lima: Ediciones Presencia Reformada, 2012), 91 (translated by the author).

[10] All Greek and Hebrew words will be transliterated in this book, instead of using the Greek and Hebrew letters.

Septuagint (the Greek translation of the Old Testament), *kajal* is normally translated as *ekklesía*.

These terms indicate that the Church is a group of people who have been called together by God. Any group of gathered Christians, wherever it is, whenever it is, represents a part of the Church. The first members of the Church were the first believers. If we assume that Adam and Eve believed the promises God made to them after the Fall, then they would be the first members of the Church.

Norberto Quesada from Cuba, where the churches have grown very fast during the last few decades, especially in small home groups, says:

> The term *ekklesía* can refer to the community or communities that meet in a home (Romans 16:5, Philemon 2), a city (Acts 8:1, 1 Corinthians 1:2) or in a province (1 Corinthians 16:19; 1 Thessalonians 2:14). Often in Paul's epistles, *ekklesía* designates the body of Christ, the totality of disciples, the universal community of believers, throughout history.
>
> ...In many passages there is a note of purpose; the church is made up of the eschatological people of God called to participate in the new age that Christ inaugurated. So *ekklesía* is more than a place. It is the people redeemed by the blood of Jesus Christ.[11]

The Church is the environment in which salvation is experienced in all its dimensions. The Fall caused the destruction of all relationships, and the Church forms a new community, a new family, where relationships between man and God and between man and his neighbor are healed.

---

[11] Norberto Quesada, doctoral thesis, chapter 1.

Definition: The Church is the body of all believers from all places in all of history.

c. The Church and the Kingdom of God

The Church is the instrument of God to establish His kingdom here on earth. This is especially seen in the Book of Acts.

Read ACTS 1:7-8.

Why do you think they asked this question? What were they expecting?

Write down the main points of Jesus' response.

Do you think Jesus answered them, or did He avoid the question?

If He answered them, what did He mean?

What does this teach us about the Kingdom of God?

Perhaps the disciples thought Jesus had misunderstood their question. They were probably expecting the restoration of Israel as an economic and military power, back to a situation similar to Israel in the time of King David. But I'm sure Jesus understood the question, and I'm sure He answered it, just not in the way they expected. The point is that yes, He will restore the Kingdom of God, but it will not be just the nation of Israel. Now it will be people of all nations. And the method for establishing the kingdom will not be war, but evangelism. The kingdom power will not be physical, but spiritual, the power of the Holy Spirit. These verses introduce the rest of the book of Acts, and provide an outline for it. The Kingdom of God will be extended, beginning in Jerusalem, then in Judea, in Samaria, and to the ends of the earth.

This means that the Church is an instrument for transforming the world. However, this transformation begins with a spiritual transformation in the heart of the individual. The changes then extend to the Church, and finally to society, to each aspect of the believer's life and to each dimension of culture.

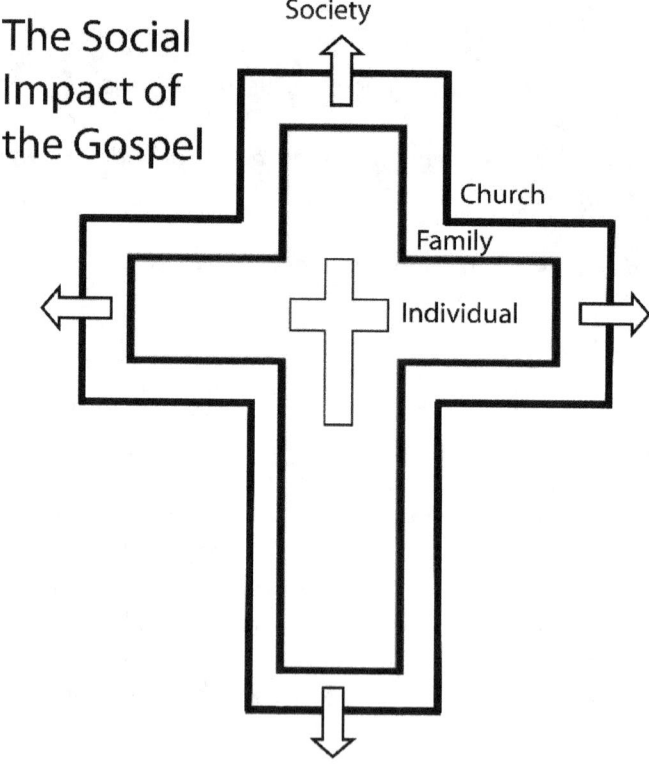

The Social Impact of the Gospel

Society

Church

Family

Individual

Pedro Arana says, "The Church sealed, empowered and guided by the Spirit, is the new creation of God, the first sign of the 'new community' that God is creating in Christ Jesus. It is the 'first fruits' of the new age."[12]

d. The Institution and the Organism

The Church is primarily an organism, a group of people. However, the church also has a visible structure; it is also an institution. Ideally, the Church would have one single structure, and would be a single world-wide organization. However, the Church has been divided into thousands of denominations. This is due to doctrinal differences and conflicts of all kinds. Some divisions have been necessary, and others have been regrettable. In any case, since this reality exists, we can't speak of "The Church" in the universal sense as one institution. Therefore, when we talk about the universal Church, we will be thinking about the Church as an organism.

e. The "Visible" Church and the "Invisible" Church

Theologians make a distinction between the "visible" church and the "invisible" church. This is not the same distinction as the one between the Church as an institution and the Church as an organism, but it is related. The "visible" church includes those who *profess* to have faith in Christ (along with their children, I would add), and the "invisible"

---

[12] Pedro Arana, 94.

church includes those who *truly* have faith and are saved. We can see who makes a profession of faith (this is "visible" to us). Usually this is seen when the person expresses his faith in words, when he is baptized, or when becomes a member of a local church. But only God knows who is truly saved. It is "invisible" to us. It is like the nation of Israel in the Old Testament; not all those who belonged to Israel externally had true faith. The same applies now to the Church; not all who outwardly belong to the Church have true faith.

The "Visible" Church and the "Invisible" Church

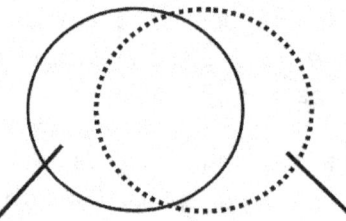

The "visible" Church (Those who profess faith and become members)

The "invisible" Church (True believers)

This means that there will always be people who make a profession of faith, but are not true believers, and there will be people who are true believers but have not become members of a local congregation (they should, but sometimes they don't). At the center is the group of true believers who have also made a profession of faith and joined a local church, which is the desired situation.

**The "Visible" Church
and the "Invisible" Church**

**The "visible" Church
(Those who profess
faith and become
members)**

**The "invisible" Church
(True believers)**

**True believers
who also belong
to the "visible" Church**

REVIEW QUESTIONS

1. According to Pedro Arana, if we describe the Church in Trinitarian terms, what is the Church?

2. What is the Greek term translated "church"? What does it mean? What two words does it come from?

3. What is the Hebrew equivalent of the Greek word for "church"? What does it mean?

4. What is the definition of the Church given in this section?

5. What is the relationship between the Church and the Kingdom of God?

6. Where does the transformation of the world begin?

7. What is the difference between the Church as an institution and the Church as an organism?

8. What is the difference between the "visible" Church and the "invisible" Church?

REFLECTION QUESTIONS

1. Why should we go to church? If a young man told you that you don't need to go to church to be OK with God, what would you say?

2. Do you consider the Church to be an instrument to change the world? How? What does this mean for the ministry of the local church?

3. How would you evaluate whether a person has made a credible profession of faith?

1.2. What is the Ministry of the Church?

Read JOHN 17:18 and 20:21.

According to these verses, God has placed us in this world to be like whom?

Our "job description" is to continue the ministry of Jesus. Of course we can't die for the sins of the world, but we can serve the Father and our neighbor out of love. Let's look at some aspects of Jesus' ministry:

Look for the following passages and note which aspects of the ministry are mentioned in them:

MATTHEW 11:25

MARK 1:35

MATTHEW 9:35 (There are three.)

MATTHEW 26:26-29

MATTHEW 26:20

We could summarize the ministry of Jesus in the following terms:

(1) Worship (Matthew 11.25)
(2) Prayer (Mark 1:35)
(3) Teaching (Matthew 9:35)
(4) The sacraments (Matthew 26:26-29)
(5) Evangelism (Matthew 9:35)

(6) Service (Matthew 9:35, healing)
(7) fellowship (Matthew 26:20)

The disciples also did the same seven things.

Read ACTS 2:42-47 and 4:31-35.

Write down the phrase or the number of the verse that suggests each aspect of ministry:

(1) Worship
(2) Prayer
(3) Teaching
(4) The sacraments
(5) Evangelism
(6) Service (helping the needy)
(7) Fellowship (being together)

To visualize these seven aspects, we could use the figure of a cross, symbolizing the fact that the ministry of Jesus is the ministry of every believer and the ministry of the Church. We are His body.

THE MINISTRY

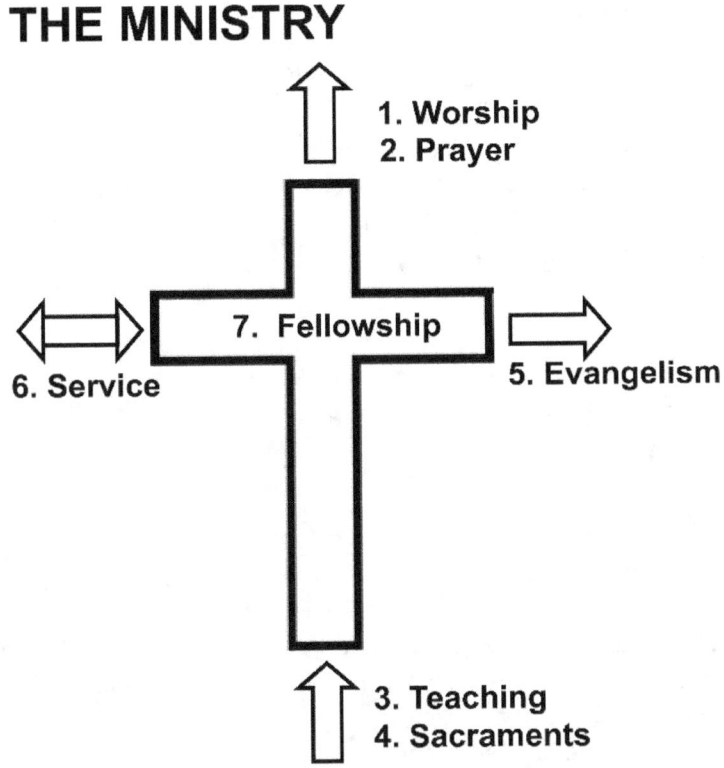

The arrows point to the object of the ministry. The church looks up to the Lord in worship and prayer. Teaching and the sacraments build the church. There are two arms extended towards the world: one is engaged in the evangelization of the unbelievers and the other arm is occupied in serving our neighbor. Note that the arrow of service also points back toward the church. Finally, the members of the church support and encourage each other as they share in fellowship.

REVIEW QUESTIONS

1. Name the seven ministries of the Church, and describe each one.

2. Draw the figure of the cross, and write the name of each ministry where it belongs, with arrows pointing toward the object of each ministry.

1.3. What is the Special Mission of Your Local Church?

The purpose of the following paragraphs is to develop a philosophy of ministry for your local church, with a special focus that fits the context in which your church is located. You will write a "mission statement" for your local church, taking into account the needs and the social and cultural characteristics of the sector.

When we started a church near the center of Santiago in Chile, our special desire was to gather people together from different backgrounds and different social levels, to show that Christ unites us. We wanted to make a contribution toward healing the problem of prejudice. On another occasion, we helped plant a church in a poor sector of Santiago where there was a lot of violence. The mission was different in the second case, with an emphasis on providing an environment of security and a sense of community. In a third church-planting project in Viña del Mar, we started a new church in a community with a higher socio-economic level. In that case, we emphasized a ministry to married couples and families, because this was where they had greater needs. In all these projects, evangelism was always the priority, because we knew that the solution to other problems depended on the spiritual transformation of people. But in each case there was a special focus, a distinct emphasis on ministry.

This special emphasis is what we include in a "mission statement." A "mission statement" describes what we want to do now, giving a unique approach to the ministry. It indicates the "personality" of your church. It should reflect biblical principles, but it should also communicate the special focus of your church.

To establish the "mission" of your particular church, a) you should investigate the needs of the neighborhood where your church is located, b) analyze the gifts and interests of the people who are involved in the ministry of your church, and c) match the needs of the neighborhood with the gifts of your people. For example, if the neighborhood's biggest problem is family conflict and the gifts of the people in your church are in the area of counseling, it is clear that the special focus of your church should be family, and that you should give priority to family-related activities, dealing with things like how to maintain a good marriage, how to raise children, and how to resolve family conflicts.

Redeemer Presbyterian Church, New York, founded by Rev. Tim Keller, expresses their mission as the following: "To spread the gospel, first through ourselves and then through the city by word, deed, and community; To bring about personal changes, social healing, and cultural renewal through a movement of churches and ministries that change New York City and through it, the world."

Some institutions also have a "motto" or "slogan" that summarizes their mission in a few words, in a phrase easy to remember. For example, for *Redeemer Presbyterian Church* it is: "Renewing the city socially, spiritually, and culturally."

It would be nice to have some way of easily remembering the mission of your church, even if it is not exactly a "motto." There is a church that uses the metaphor of a house, and always speaks of three words to describe its mission: "lobby, kitchen, and living room". The "lobby" represents how they will make people feel comfortable and at home. The "kitchen" symbolizes the spiritual nourishment they will give them. The "living room" points to the fact that they experience fellowship and form friendships. Another church speaks of the "bases" of baseball. Each base (first, second, and third) represents a different stage of discipleship.

REVIEW QUESTIONS

1. Explain what the "mission statement" of a church is.

2. Explain what the "motto" of a church is.

EXERCISE

Write a mission statement for your church. First, analyze the needs of your church neighborhood, analyze the gifts of the people involved in your church, and consider biblical principles. Pray for the Lord's guidance, then write up a mission statement to propose to the leaders of your church. This helps set priorities (we can't do everything!) and gives a unique identity to your church. Why does your church exist? What is its special emphasis? The statement should be brief and clear. Then write a "motto" for your church.

Mission Statement:

Motto:

1.4 Church Government

The people of God began in the form of a family, or a tribe. This is especially clear in the time of Abraham, when God made a covenant with him, promising to bless his family. They continued in this form, moving from one country to another, until the time of Moses, when they had grown much larger. After they left Egypt, they conquered the land of Palestine and established themselves as a nation. Throughout the rest of the Old Testament, the history of God's people is the history of the nation of Israel. In the New Testament, the people of God becomes the Church, which includes Gentiles and believers of all nations. Since the people of God is no longer one single political nation, the form of government changes.

The book of Acts narrates how the New Testament Church grew as they multiplied in small local congregations that normally met in houses. We see the selection and appointment of local leaders, and also the beginnings of a relationship among the different local congregations. Acts gives us some guidelines about how the Church should be governed. However, what occurs in history is not necessarily normative, and there are differences of opinion among denominations about exactly how church government should be structured.

Historically, there have been three basic forms of ecclesiastical government, which we will call "Episcopal," "Congregationalist," and "Presbyterian." In all three cases, they agree that Christ is the head of the church, that the church has human leaders, that all the members participate somehow, and that our unity should be expressed somehow, but they have different governing structures.

In the "Episcopal" structure, there is a strong hierarchy of authority. The congregation does not participate in the selection of who will be their pastor or priest. Instead, it is decided by their superior authorities, who are usually called *bishops* ("epískopos" in Greek, which means "overseer"). The Roman Catholic Church is the most notable example of this structure, in which the Pope is the highest authority. The Greek Orthodox Church, the Lutheran Church, the Methodist Church, and the Anglican Church, are also considered "Episcopal" in their government. The figure below illustrates this structure. Notice the arrow indicating that the authority is exercised from top to bottom. The advantages of the Episcopal system are that it reflects unity and it encourages accountability.

Episcopal Form of Church Government (Roman Catholic version)

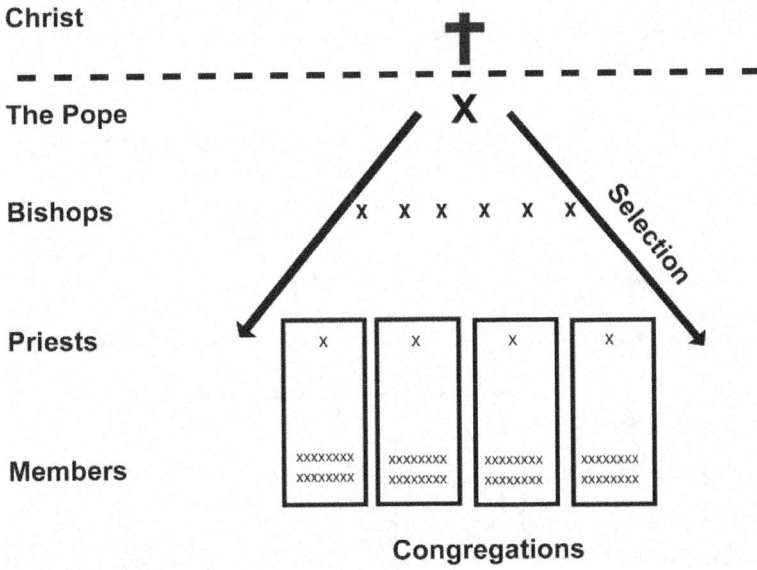

Congregations

In the "Congregationalist" system, normally used for example in most Baptist churches, the authority rests in the congregation itself, and each congregation is independent. Andreas Köstenberger says, "At the heart of Congregationalism is the belief that local congregations are to govern their own affairs." The members of the congregation select who will be their pastor. They usually have a group of leaders who work with him, called "deacons" or "elders," who are also elected by the congregation. The authority given to the elected leaders varies among their churches. According to Köstenberger, "the spectrum reaches all the way from a full-fledged democratic model on the one hand to elder rule on the other, with various forms of church leadership and congregational rule or participation in between these two extremes." The key is that there is no outside governing body over the congregation. Notice in the figure the arrows indicating that the human authority is exercised upward. The advantage of the Congregationalist system is the freedom it gives each congregation.[13]

Congregationalist Church Government

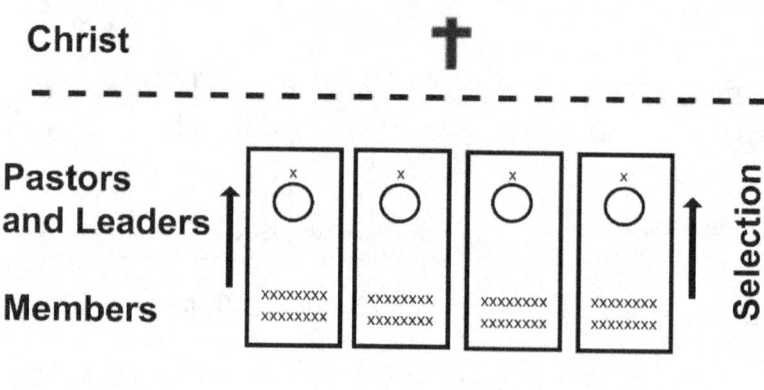

The Presbyterian system includes authority from both above and below. (Notice in the figure below the arrows pointing in both directions.) The process of selecting leaders involves both a supervising group of already-elected leaders

---

[13] Andreas Körstenberger, "Church Government: Congregationalism". https://www.biblicalfoundations.org/church-government-congregationalism/ (8/14/2019).

and the participation of the people whose leader is being chosen.

The local church is governed by a body of "elders" or "presbyters," who are elected by the congregation. This group is usually called a "session." Members of the congregation can propose candidates for elders, but the already-elected elders must approve them. The session itself can also propose candidates. The final step is the vote by the congregation. A pastor is chosen in much the same way, but it also involves the supervision of a superior ecclesiastical body, as explained below. The pastor is the moderator of the local session.

Up to this point, the structure of some Congregationalist churches might seem similar. But there is a big difference:

In the Presbyterian system, above the local churches is a supervising body called a "presbytery", composed of pastors and elders from a group of local churches, usually a group within a geographical area.

Furthermore, above all the presbyteries is a "Synod," or "General Assembly," which consists of representative pastors and elders from all churches in the whole country.

Going back to the selection of a pastor, in the Presbyterian system, before a pastor can become ordained and become a candidate for a church, he must be examined and approved by a presbytery. Only then can he be invited by a congregation to be their pastor. Furthermore, the presbytery must approve any particular call of a pastor to a congregation.

Note that in this case, the authority rests in groups of people (represented by circles in the figure), and not in individuals, as in the Episcopal system. In addition, the members of the lower bodies participate in the selection of the members of the higher bodies. The Presbyterians would like to keep the advantages of both of the other systems by expressing unity and encouraging accountability, but also preserving a degree of independence in each local congregation.

Presbyterian Church Government

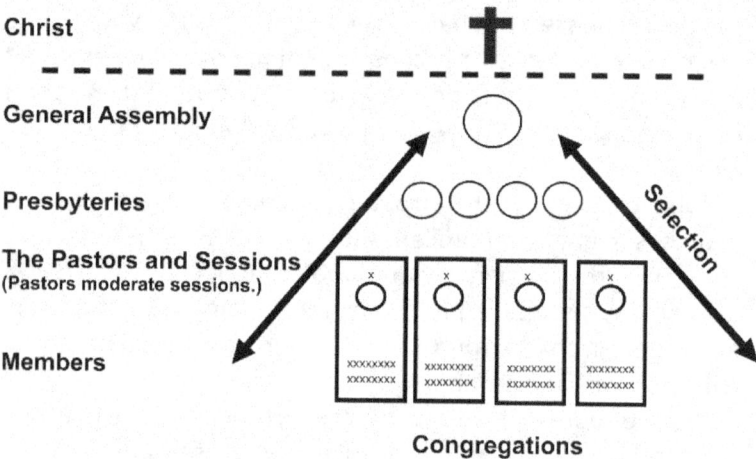

Congregations

The New Testament gives us some details about how the Church was organized, and how the local churches were organized. I think it's good to follow those examples. However, as mentioned above, the history of the Church in New Testament times is not necessarily normative in every respect. That is, not everything they did at that time constitutes general ethical principles for all churches everywhere. If there is no clear endorsement of an action in the didactic passages of the New Testament (such as in the epistles), we should not insist on making a universal principle out it.

Read the following passages to see what you can learn from them about church government:

ACTS 6:5-6

Who voted to elect the deacons?

Who supervised the process?

Who placed their hands on them to install them officially?

Here we see a combination of supervision on the part of the apostles and participation in the selection process by the congregation.

ACTS 15:2

This was the first church council, called to deal with the problem in Antioch.

Where was this meeting held?

Who participated?

Where were the participants from?

Did this council express any authority over other churches? Did they make any decisions that affected other churches?

1 PETER 5:2-3

What is the warning about leadership?

We can draw the following conclusions from these passages:

In the New Testament churches,...

1. The members participated in the selection of their leaders.
2. The already-existing leaders supervised the local churches and the process of selecting new leaders.
3. Leaders from various congregations participated in a council that affected those congregations.
4. There was a sense of unity among the churches.
5. They did not establish a hierarchical structure of officers that could exercise authority on their own.

While these historical examples are not meant to be moral imperatives, I think it is best to try to implement a system of government that includes these elements somehow.

REVIEW QUESTIONS

1. What are the three basic forms of church government?

2. Explain the differences between these forms of government.

REFLECTION QUESTIONS

1. What is the system of government of your church? Does it reflect what we observe in the churches in the book of Acts?

2. What do you think? What kind of government should churches have?

Recommended Additional Reading

Berkhof, Louis. *Systematic Theology*, New Combined Edition, part 5, "The Doctrine of the Church and the Means of Grace," section 2, "Nature of the Church". Grand Rapids: Eerdmans, 1996.

Grudem, Wayne. *Systematic Theology*, part 6, "The Doctrine of the Church," chapters 44-48. Leicester, England: Inter-Varsity Press / Grand Rapids: Zondervan, 1994.

Chapter 2: Our Vision; the Kingdom of God

If you want to build a ship,
don't drum up people together to collect wood
and don't assign them tasks and work,
but rather teach them to long for the endless immensity of the sea.

Attributed to Antoine de Saint-Exupéry.[14]

Previously we talked about the "mission" of the local church. Now let's look at the bigger picture, the "vision" for our ministry. While a mission statement expresses what we want to do *now*, a "vision statement" describes the ideal outcome we want to see in the *future*. For example, Microsoft's "vision" is: "A computer on every desk and in every home." Notice the difference: This phrase does not describe what you do now to realize the vision, but what you want to see someday. The vision encourages people to fulfill the mission now, because everyone knows where they are going. So what is the vision of the Church? Where are we going? According to the Bible, the big picture is called the Kingdom of God.

There is an anecdote about three workers during the Middle Ages. Someone saw them working and approached them to see what they were doing. When he asked the first,

---

[14] Quoted in *The Forgotten Ways*, by Alan Hirsch (Grand Rapids: Brazos Press, 2006), who attributes the quote to Antoine de Saint-Exupéry. But this is probably an indirect or imprecise quote. See: <http://quoteinvestigator.com/2015/08/25/sea/> (July 18, 2017)

"Sir, can you tell me what you are doing?", the worker replied, "I am laying bricks." When he approached the second to ask the same question, he said, "I'm making a wall." Finally, when he asked the third, he replied with great pride, "I am building a cathedral!"[15]

Do you tend to think almost exclusively about your own personal ministry (laying bricks)? Do you only think about your local church (building a wall)? Or do you see how your ministry fits into the bigger picture, the divine project, which is the Kingdom of God (the cathedral)?

Read MATTHEW 4:23.

How is the preaching of Jesus summarized here?

Our general vision is to establish the Kingdom of God. This theme describes what God is doing all throughout the Bible. As we study the meaning of the Kingdom of God, we will see the ultimate goal. Afterwards, we will see how to apply this to the local church.

2.1. The Kingdom of God

What is the Kingdom of God? Think of a political realm today. What does it include? It includes land, people, rulers, and laws to guide them. In a similar way, the Kingdom of God is a people, a place, a sovereign ruler, who is God, and a covenant to guide their relationship. The Kingdom of God

---

[15] This story is found many places. According to the following site of "Harvard Magazine", the original author is Peter Drucker. <http://harvardmagazine.com/breaking-news/three-stonecutters-the-future-business-education> (Oct. 14, 2015).

involves all of society, every aspect of life. The Kingdom of God is all that happens where God is reigning. It is manifest wherever and whenever His will is done.

There is an individualistic tendency in our society today, and it has heavily influenced our churches. We tend to talk about salvation primarily in terms of how it affects each one of us personally. But in the Bible, God has a relationship with his people as a body. He makes covenants with them as a responsible unit. The Kingdom of God is a family, a community.

Another tendency is to separate the secular and the spiritual, leaving some aspects of life as if they were "neutral". I remember talking to a young lady who worked in the office of a municipality in Santiago, Chile. I asked her what she did all day at work. She told me that she spent the day writing letters and reports. I said, "How do you think you glorify God in your work?" She replied, "Well, I try to talk to my co-workers about my faith, and I try to be kind to them." I continued, "That's good, but in the work itself, when you are writing the reports, how does that glorify God?" She didn't know what to say. Then I asked her what the municipality does. She explained that they were building houses for the poor and helping to solve problems in the community. I asked her if her reports were part of the process of helping those in need, and she said yes. "You see?," I said, "even when you're writing tedious reports, you're glorifying God, because those reports are important for helping a lot of people." She had not thought about it before, but agreed. I think everyone should take the time to analyze how their work glorifies God. We should keep the big picture in mind. Although our work may seem "secular," because it is not an activity of the Church, it is actually part of the Kingdom of God.

REVIEW QUESTIONS

1. What is a "vision statement"?

2. What is the general vision of the Church?

3. What is the kingdom of God?

4. What are the two erroneous tendencies that are corrected by a proper concept of the kingdom of God?

REFLECTION QUESTIONS

1. How do you see your ministry or your work (even if it is a "secular" job) connected to the larger vision of building the Kingdom of God?

2. Does it change the way you feel about your ministry or work to see it as part of establishing the kingdom of God?

2.2. The Cultural Mandate and the Great Commission

These two overarching biblical themes give us a theological basis for understanding the vision for our ministry.

a. The Cultural Mandate

Before the Fall, God gave an important command to man:

And God blessed them. And God said to them, "Be fruitful and multiply and fill the earth and subdue it, and have dominion over the fish of the sea and over the birds of the heavens and over every living thing that moves on the earth." **GENESIS 1:28**

God put Adam and Eve in the garden to take care of it. He brought them the animals so that they could give them names. He left them in charge.

Yet you have made him a little lower than the heavenly beings and crowned him with glory and honor. You have given him dominion over the works of your hands; you have put all things under his feet. **PSALM 8:5-6**

Managing the creation involves much more than caring for plants. To "subdue" it, man has to organize things and create the necessary social structures. He has to maintain order as the population multiplies. Without sin, man would have developed a complex and orderly society, a healthy culture, and social organizations that functioned well. Genesis 1:28 has been called "the Cultural Mandate," because God's command includes developing all of society and culture according to His will. We could also say that this is a mandate to establish the Kingdom of God.

Unfortunately, because of sin and the Fall, man can no longer fulfill the Cultural Mandate, he can no longer establish the Kingdom of God, without a supernatural work of redemption. Man's heart must be transformed before he can transform the world. So it shouldn't surprise us to see that the central theme of the Bible is salvation in Christ.

b. The Great Commission

The Great Commission (Matthew 28:18-20) has now become the first step in fulfilling the Cultural Mandate, the first step in establishing the Kingdom of God.

> *All authority in heaven and on earth has been given to me. Go therefore and make disciples of all nations, baptizing them in the name of the Father and of the Son and of the Holy Spirit, teaching them to observe all that I have commanded you. And behold, I am with you always, to the end of the age.* **MATTHEW 28.18-20**

Salvation includes all aspects of life. Everything that was destroyed in the Fall will be restored. Each dimension of conflict will be healed: between man and God, between man and his neighbor, between man and nature, and between man and his own heart.

> *For in him all the fullness of God was pleased to dwell, and through him to reconcile to himself all things, whether on earth or in heaven, making peace by the blood of his cross.* **COLOSSIANS 1:19-20**

When a person believes the gospel and trusts Jesus for his salvation, his whole life is transformed. Then he or she can work toward transforming all of society for the glory of God.

It is as if an artist had been commissioned to paint something beautiful (the Cultural Mandate), but then becomes blind (the Fall). He needs to be healed and recover his sight first (salvation through the Great Commission). And when he recovers his sight, he begins to paint again! He doesn't just sit there and wait to be taken to heaven when he dies.

Jesus taught us to pray, "Hallowed be thy name, thy kingdom come: thy will be done on earth as it is in heaven" (Matthew 6:10). The Kingdom of God includes the growth of the Church through evangelization, but it also includes the transformation of the world.

REVIEW QUESTIONS

1. What is the "Cultural Mandate"?

2. What is the "Great Commission"?

REFLECTION QUESTIONS

1. In your own life, in what specific ways can you work toward fulfilling the Great Commission and the Cultural Mandate?

2. How can your church work toward fulfilling the Great Commission and the Cultural Mandate?

2.3. The Kingdom of God in the Old Testament

Read GENESIS 17:4-8.

What are the promises of the covenant God made with Abraham?

We can summarize the promises, using the letter "P" for each one. God promises:

> A people (a multitude, v. 5),
> His presence (to be his God, vv. 7, 8), and
> A place (Canaan, v. 8)

The key words are:

> **P**eople
> **P**resence
> **P**lace

The history of Israel in the Old Testament exhibits the fulfillment of these promises and then the loss of these blessings.

People
Fulfillment: The nation of Israel is formed.
Loss: Israel is divided and loses her identity when conquered.

Presence
Fulfillment: God manifests Himself especially in the tabernacle and the temple.
Loss: The temple is destroyed and God removes His blessing.

Place
Fulfillment: God gives them the land of Canaan.
Loss: The country is conquered and dominated by foreigners.

The failures and the losses point to the need for Christ. He will come and keep the covenant perfectly, and He will suffer the punishment that God's people deserve for NOT having kept the covenant.

The most important fulfillment of the promises made to Abraham was not temporal and material, but eternal and spiritual.

Read HEBREWS 11:8-10.

What was Abraham really looking for?

It's important to see our own connection with the people of God from the Old Testament.

Read HEBREWS 11:39-40.

Did the heroes of the faith see the final fulfillment of the promises?

Why?

God was waiting for us to be included before fulfilling all the promises! This means that we are all connected throughout all history and in all places! From the time of Adam until Christ returns, from Chile to Siberia!

Finally, notice the direction of the evangelistic movement in the Old Testament. In science, they speak of "centripetal" force, towards the center (like the force of gravity) and "centrifugal" force, outwards.

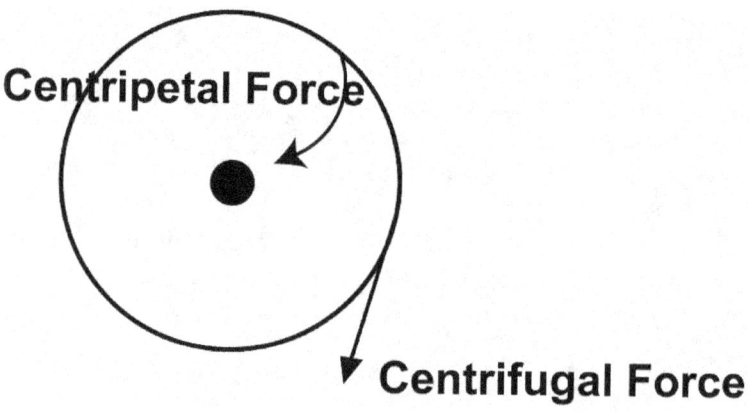

What was the emphasis in the time of the Old Testament? Outward or inward?

To be a member of God's people, a man had to be circumcised, become a Jew, and participate in temple festivals and ceremonies. This indicates primarily a centripetal movement, towards the center.

However, we see indications of a change in the time of the Babylonian captivity. Since they could not go to the temple in Jerusalem, they established synagogues throughout the Mediterranean. By necessity, they could not focus only on one central location.

REVIEW QUESTIONS

1. What were the three promises God made to Abram?

2. Summarize how the Old Testament promises were fulfilled, then the blessings were lost.

3. Why did the heroes of the faith not receive the final fulfillment of the promises?

4. Was the evangelistic force of the Old Testament mostly inward or outward?

REFLECTION QUESTIONS

1. What does it mean to you to know that you are connected with other members of the kingdom of God throughout history and throughout the world?

2. Does your church exercise more of a centrifugal force or more of a centripetal evangelistic force?

2.4. The Kingdom of God in the New Testament

Read MATTHEW 4:17.

What is "at hand"?

Why is it at hand now?

Who is the king?

Read MATTHEW 28:18-20.

In what direction is the evangelistic thrust now? Inward or outward? Centripetal or centrifugal?

Read ACTS 1:6-8.

What ministry has the priority in establishing the kingdom of God?

From whom does the power come to extend the kingdom?

In what direction is the kingdom going to grow, inward or outward?

Growth was not only numerical. It was not just a matter of "saving souls." It also affected the lives of those who became Christians, and made an impact on society.

Read ACTS 2:42-47 and ACTS 4:32-35.

What changes do you see in these passages?

Another radical change was the way in which different types of people (different social classes and different ethnic groups) were united in the same Church. Part of the "outward" movement is the ability to accept those who are different. The "emerging Church" movement warns that we are losing new people because we do not go out to seek them, and because we do not accept people who are different. They argue that in many churches, residents of the surrounding sector are not like the members of the church in many social and cultural aspects. Therefore, when they approach the church, they don't feel comfortable.[16]

Read REVELATION 5:9-10.

How is diversity of the kingdom reflected here?

Read REVELATION 21:1-5.

What will the eternal form of the kingdom be like?

What aspects will be changed? Only "spiritual" aspects?

What things will be made new?

We can summarize the fulfillment of the covenant promises in the time of the New Testament, and in the time when Jesus returns:

People
NT: The people of God is the Church, believers from all nations.
Return: All believers from all places and all times, sanctified and glorified.

Presence
NT: Jesus Himself is present, and then sends the Holy Spirit to live in the hearts of all believers.

---

[16] *The Forgotten Ways*, Alan Hirsch (Grand Rapids: Brazos Press, 2006), chapter 1.

Return: We will all see Jesus face to face in His glory.

Place
NT: The kingdom of God is extended to all the earth.
Return: We will have new heavens and a new earth, where we will live eternally.

Our churches should be a foretaste of the eternal stage of the kingdom. They should manifest, even though imperfectly, the characteristics of the glorified people of God.

REVIEW QUESTIONS

1. How were the covenant promises fulfilled at the time of the New Testament?

2. How will the promises be fulfilled when Jesus returns?

3. In what direction is the evangelistic force at the time of Jesus?

2.5. The Kingdom of God in the History of the Church

The Kingdom of God has continued to grow throughout history. The purpose of this section is to encourage you as you see the Lord's work in the world, observing both numerical growth and the impact on society. We will make brief observations about the history of the Church up until the time of the Reformation, and then take a quick look at the current world situation.

a. 100-310 A.D.

Some estimate that there were only about 25,000 Christians in the world around 100 A.D., and that there were about 20 million by 310.[17] Growth was almost all in the Mediterranean area. At first, they met in houses (1 Corinthians 16:19 and Colossians 4:15). During the first few centuries, they were heavily persecuted.

---

[17] Alan Hirsch, *Forgotten Ways* (Grand Rapids: Brazos Press, 2006).

Early Christians made an impression by the way they lived their lives. Someone wrote at the end of the second century:

> They live in their own countries as though they were only passing through. They play their full role as citizens, but labor under all the disabilities of aliens....They live in the flesh, but they are not governed by the desires of the flesh. They pass their days upon earth, but they are citizens of heaven. Obedient to the laws, they yet live on a level that transcends the law. Christians love all men, but all men persecute them.[18]

b. 310-800 A.D.

When Constantine (the Roman emperor between 306-337) allegedly was converted in 312, the situation changed for Christians. He gave his blessing to Christianity (Edict of Milan, 313), and the Church grew and increased its influence in society. Since they no longer had to meet in private, they began to build cathedrals.

What do you think the cathedrals meant for the evangelistic force? Would it become more inward or outward?

---

[18] From *A Letter to Diognetus* (Nn. 5-6; Funk, 397-401), probably from the end of the second century, <http://www.vatican.va/spirit/documents/spirit_20010522_diogneto_en.html>

Between Constantine and the Reformation, the Church continued to grow in Europe in general. However, there were many struggles regarding doctrine and practice in this period. For example, they struggled to express the doctrine of the Trinity and to combat pelagianism, which minimized the effects of the Fall. The authority of the Pope continued to grow.

In the 7th century, growth declined. Why? There were two main reasons: the growth of Islam, which began in 610, and a theological conflict about the Holy Spirit. The Eastern Church did not want to include in the creeds the phrase that says that the Holy Spirit also proceeds from the Son, not just from the Father.

See the map below of the growth of Christianity until 800 AD:

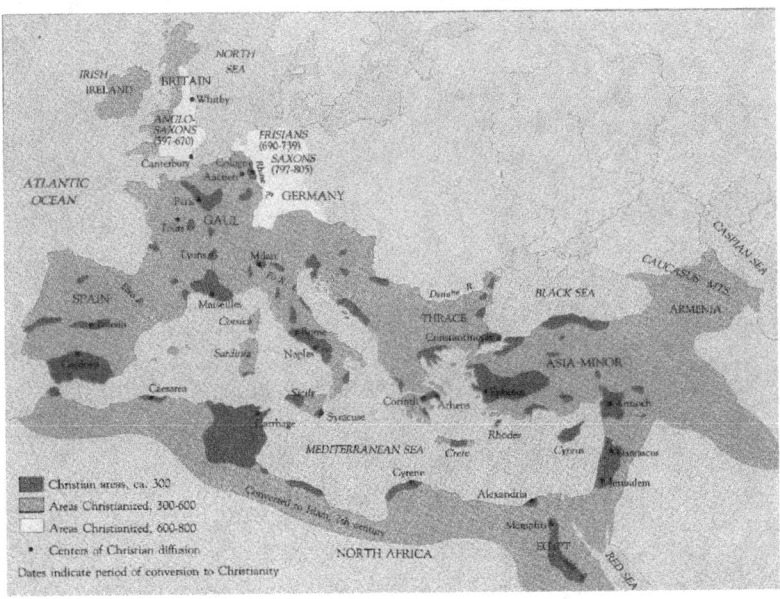

19

Dark: Until 300 AD (Small areas around Mediterranean)
Lighter: 300-600 AD (Most of Europe, Mediterranean coast)
Very light: 600-800 AD (Germany, England)

REVIEW QUESTIONS

1. Some estimate that in the year 100 AD, there were about _____ Christians in the world, and that by the year 310, there were around _____.

2. In what geographic areas did the Church grow most during the first three centuries?

3. Where did people usually meet for worship services during the first few centuries?

4. What happened in the fourth century that changed the relation between the Church and society?

5. Why did the Church grow more slowly in the 7th century?

REFLECTION QUESTIONS

1. What factors contributed to the growth of the Church in the first centuries?

2. What can we learn from this period of church history?

---

[19] <www.usu.edu/markdamen/1320hist&Civ/chapters/13XITY.htm>

c. The Division of 1054

The controversy regarding whether the Holy Spirit also "proceeded" from the Son continued, and became one of the causes of the eventual split between the Roman Catholic Church and the Eastern Orthodox Church in 1054. The conflict was not just about the doctrine itself, but about the way in which the Western Church had modified the Nicene Creed. According to the Eastern Church, they violated the agreement made in the Council of Ephesus in 451, forbidding any addition to the creed.[20]

The other cause of the division was the power struggle between Rome and Constantinople. Who has the true authority over the Church? The culmination of this conflict was that both the Pope in Rome and the Patriarch of Constantinople mutually excommunicated each other.[21]

Shortly after this division, the Crusades were initiated (1095) as an attempt to take back the Holy Lands from Muslim rule. After two centuries, the efforts failed. Strangely, during one of the crusades, in 1204, the armies sacked Constantinople, resulting in even deeper division between the Catholic and the Orthodox churches.[22] None of this makes an attractive picture of church growth.

---

[20] "Filioque," <https://orthodoxwiki.org/Filioque> Feb. 8, 2018.

[21] "Schism of 1054",
<https://www.britannica.com/event/Schism-of-1054> Feb. 8, 2018.

[22] See articles in *Wikipedia* on "Crusades" and "Sack of Constantinople."

d. The Reformation

The causes of the Reformation were multiple. Many saw corruption in the Roman Catholic Church, and objected to practices such as selling "indulgences". (For donations, they promised that the temporal punishment for sins would be removed.) In 1517, Martin Luther posted his *95 Theses* on the door of the chapel in Wittenberg, expressing his complaints, and the moment became known as the beginning of the Reformation. Luther was later excommunicated.

The most important cause of the Reformation was doctrinal. Protestants disagreed with the Roman Catholic Church on important issues, often summarized in what are known as the "solas." Some speak of three "solas" and others speak of five. The earliest list of three includes: 1) *Sola Scriptura*. Scripture is our only authority, not Scripture and Tradition. 2) *Sola Fide*. Salvation is received by faith alone, not by faith and works and the sacraments. 3) *Sola Gratia*. We are saved only by the grace of God, not by grace and merits. Later lists include: 4) *Solus Christus*. Jesus is our only mediator between man and God, not Jesus and Mary and the saints. 5) *Soli Deo Gloria*. We should glorify God alone.

How did the kingdom of God grow during the time of the reformation? Some people may have the impression that the Reformers were only academic theologians, but they actually promoted evangelism and made great efforts to transform society. From Geneva, missionaries were sent to France, Holland, Hungary, Italy, Poland, and Brazil.[23]   Philip

---

[23] Frank A. James III (RTS Orlando), "Calvin the Evangelist" Nov. 11, 2014. <http://rq.rts.edu/fall01/james.html>,

Edgcumbe Hughes says that Geneva was a "school of missions ... and a dynamic center of missionary activity".[24]

In Geneva, Calvin preached and taught, but under his leadership they also received refugees, helped the poor, cared for the elderly, and established hospitals. They changed the laws to improve trade, and installed a sewer system. They literally cleaned up the city!

The Reformation made a big impact on many dimensions of society. The reformers developed a Christian worldview, eliminating the distinction between "sacred" and "secular". They taught what has been called the "Protestant work ethic," encouraging people to be responsible and to take initiative. They supported science and research, and motivated people to develop the artistic gifts that God has given us. Calvin said:

> The invention of the arts, and other things which serve the common use and convenience of life, is a gift of God by no means to be despised, and a faculty worthy of commendation.[25]

e. The World Today

There is still much to do, and many people to reach, but the Church is growing more than ever! A 2011 report says that one-third of the world is "Christian" (2.18 billion, without distinguishing between denominations).

---

[24] Frank A. James III, "Calvin the Evangelist".

[25] John Calvin, Commentary on Genesis, vol. 1 (Grand Rapids: Christian Classics Ethereal Library), s.v. Genesis 4:20, p. 148. <https://www.ccel.org/ccel/calvin/calcom01.html> (July 18, 2017)

The concentration has changed radically. In 1910, 2/3 of the world's Christians still lived in Europe. One hundred years later, in the year 2010, only 1/4 lived in Europe. Now more than 1/3 of the Christians are in the Americas.[26] Latin America continues to experience growth, especially in countries like Cuba, the Dominican Republic, Guatemala and Nicaragua.

Africa is seeing amazing growth: in 1900, there were 10 million "Christians" (without distinguishing Catholics and Protestants), and by 2000, there were 360 million.[27]

China is another striking example. One source says that in the 1940s, there were around two million Christians in China. When they were being persecuted, many thought that they would stop growing. However, by the end of the 1970s, there were almost 80 million![28] (The statistics vary widely, perhaps because of the difference between the "underground" church, which is difficult to measure, and official church figures recognized by the government.) In this case, 80% of the Christians are Protestants.[29]

In Iran, in 1972, there were only 200 (yes, there were 200, not 2,000, not 200,000!) Christians from a Muslim background. In the year 2012, there were 370,000. [30]

---

[26] "Global Christianity," 11/12/2014. < http://www.pewforum.org/2011/12/19/global-christianity-exec/>

[27] Charles Colson, "How Christianity is Growing Around the World," <http://www.cbn.com/spirituallife/biblestudyandtheology/perspectives/colson020722.aspx>, 12/11/2014.

[28] Alan Hirsch, *Forgotten Ways.*

[29] "Christianity in its Global Context"

[30] Christian Post World <http://www.christianpost.com/news/open-doors-growth-of-christianity-in-iran-explosive-71946/> 11/11/14

Christianity is still the largest religion in the world (counting Catholics and Orthodox Christians). See the map below.

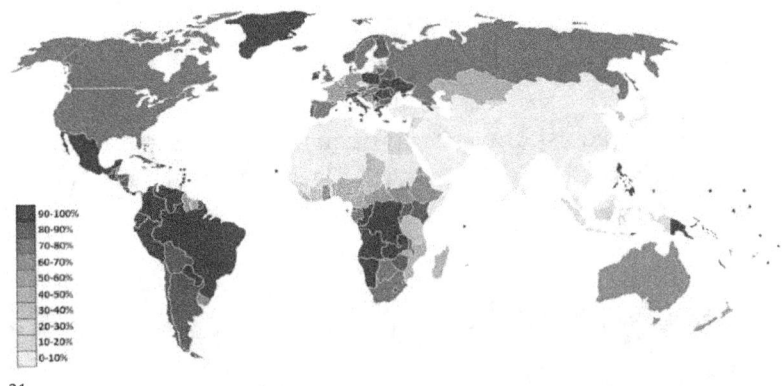

31

The colors indicate the percentage of professing Christians in each country. The darker the color, the greater the percentage. The darkest color represents 90-100%. The countries of the Middle East and northern Africa are predominantly Muslim.

What about the transformation of society? While much remains to improve, we have seen a lot of progress. A report of *Gordon Conwell Seminary* concludes that Christians are doing more now to help solve world problems.[32]

Conclusion

The Lord is doing more than some of us might have imagined to establish His kingdom!

---

[31] https://www.saberespractico.com/curiosidades/religion-mayoritaria-en-el-mundo/ (Feb. 14, 2019)
[32] "Christianity in its Global Context"

Orientation for Leaders

Read 2 KINGS 6:15-17.

Why was Elisha's servant afraid?

What happened when Elisha prayed that the Lord open his servants eyes? What did he see?

We should ask the Lord to open our eyes to see what He is doing in the world. We are NOT losing the war! The Church is NOT dying!

REVIEW QUESTIONS

1. What were the causes of the division in 1054 AD?

2. What were the causes of the Reformation?

3. What were Calvin's efforts to promote missions?

4. What was the social impact of Calvin's ministry in Geneva?

5. In general, what were some of the social changes that the Reformation brought?

6. What percentage of the world considers themselves Christians today?

7. What is the largest religion in the world?

REFLECTION QUESTIONS

1. What can we learn from the example of Calvin and the reformers about fulfilling the Great Commission and the Cultural Mandate?

2. What can we learn from this period of church history about church growth?

3. Do you have a sense of participating in something big when you help in the ministry of the Church?

2.6. The Vision of Your Local Church

After noting that the general vision of the Church is to establish the kingdom of God, and after reviewing what it is and how it has grown throughout history, you can make a more specific statement about how you would like to see your local church make an impact for the kingdom of God. Remember that a "vision statement" points to the ideal future. What is your dream for your city? For your county? For the world? Try to think of the larger impact, starting with your local church and extending to the world. This kind of vision is something you may never see in your lifetime, but it gives you direction, and it will hopefully keep you encouraged. Remember the example of Microsoft: they wanted to see a computer on every desk and in every home.

EXERCISE

Write a "vision statement" for your local church, thinking of the impact it could have in your city, in your country, and in the whole world.

Recommended Additional Reading

Gonzalez, Justo L. *The Story of Christianity*, 2 volumes. New York: HarperCollins, 2010.

Hirsch, Alan. *Forgotten Ways*. Grand Rapids: Brazos Press, 2006.

Chapter 3: Our Leaders; Their Characteristics and Call

Because grace runs downhill,
it is very important that you not
stake out your territory
at the top of the hill.[33]

Steve Brown

All members of the local church should be "ministers," but some have special tasks, including the task of training others (Ephesians 4:12). We will call these people who train others "leaders." But they are also "servants," and are not to "domineer over" the others (1 Peter 5:2-3). If you are not claiming a position of leadership so that you can be "on top of the hill," as Steve Brown says, you will receive the grace you need to carry out the tasks that the Lord gives you.

In this chapter, we will analyze how God calls and prepares leaders. Gifts and abilities are important, but not as important as spiritual character.

Pedro Arana speaks about "disciplers":

> We should ask the Lord of the Church that He give to all of us who are *disciplers*, beginning with the pastors, presbyters, deacons, Sunday School teachers, and youth leaders, a *pastoral heart* to fulfill

---

[33] Steve Brown, *A Scandalous Freedom*, (West Monroe, Louisiana: Howard Publishing Company, 2004), 101.

our ministry, not only to communicate the truth of God in concepts, but also to be sensitive to the spiritual and human needs of the new believers....[34]

3.1. Elders, Pastors, and Deacons

We will examine the meaning of the offices that are mentioned in the New Testament. Technically, there are only two: elder (sometimes called presbyter) and deacon. But we will also include pastors as a special kind of elder.

a. Elder

The word "elder," or "presbyter," is the translation of the Greek word "presbíteros" in the New Testament, and of the Hebrew word "zaqen" in the Old Testament. These terms mean literally "an older man" or "elder."

Among many ancient peoples, like the Egyptians (Genesis 50:7), the Moabites and the Midianites for example (Numbers 22:7), the older men exercised supervising roles. They had more experience, and were naturally respected as leaders.

It was the same in Israel. There was no age limit stipulated to qualify as an "elder." The first time the name appears among the Israelites is at the time of Moses, when they were still in Egypt. Exodus 3:16 says: "Go and gather the elders of Israel together...." It seems to be something so natural that it didn't need explanation. Then in Exodus 24:1, God tells Moses to go up with "seventy of the elders" to Mount Sinai.

---

[34] Pedro Arana, *Iniciación*, xiii.

The elders carried a lot of influence. According to the laws given to Moses, cities in the Promised Land were to have elders that governed them, sometimes acting like judges (Deuteronomy 19:12, 21:2, 22:15, 25:7). The elders asked for a king for Israel (1 Samuel 8:4), and later anointed David. During the monarchy, they gave counsel to other kings (1 Kings 20:7-8).

By the time of Jesus, the elders formed part of the Sanhedrin, the governing body of the Jews. In fact, tradition considered the origin of the Sanhedrin to be when the seventy elders went up to Sinai with Moses.[35] In the gospels and in Acts, they are frequently mentioned in the same phrase with the chief priests, speaking of key Jewish leaders (Matthew 21:23, Acts 4:8 and 23).

When the New Testament churches were being established, the word *presbíteros* began to be used as a technical term for their officers. The church in Jerusalem had a group of elders that functioned somewhat like the leaders of the synagogues, and somewhat like the Sanhedrin.[36] In the council of Jerusalem, they are named in the same phrase with the apostles: "the apostles and the elders were gathered together to consider this matter" (Acts 15:6).

Read TITUS 1:5-9.

Why did Paul leave Titus in Crete? (v. 5)

---

[35] Thompson, J. A. (1996). Sanhedrin. In D. R. W. Wood, I. H. Marshall, A. R. Millard, J. I. Packer, & D. J. Wiseman (Eds.), *New Bible dictionary* (3rd ed., p. 1060). Leicester, England; Downers Grove, IL: InterVarsity Press.

[36] Kittel, G., Friedrich, G., & Bromiley, G. W. *Theological Dictionary of the New Testament* (Grand Rapids, MI: W.B. Eerdmans, 1985), 932.

What other two terms are used for elders in verse 7?

The word in verse 7 that is sometimes translated "overseer" and sometimes as "bishop" is *epískopos* in Greek. It means "supervisor," "superintendent," or "overseer." It is clear in the context and literary structure that this term was not meant to be a technical term for another separate office, different from an elder, but is used rather as a synonym of elder.

What can we learn about the role of the elder from this passage?

What are the characteristics of an elder?

If you have a problem with any of these characteristics, or if you have another moral problem, you should speak with the pastor or church leader before accepting a call to the office of presbyter. This is not a complete list, but it gives some guidelines. It leads us to examine some aspects of our life, and it moves us to pray that the Lord will help us grow in these areas. Also, if you have been selected to be an elder, you should not be proud of your level of spirituality. Spiritual arrogance is also a sin, and we must always recognize our weaknesses and our total dependence on the Lord. "Therefore let anyone who thinks that he stands take heed lest he fall" (1 Corinthians 10:12).

Some of these characteristics in Titus 1 need a little explanation:

1) *Above reproach*

The word in Greek means that he is free from accusations. It means that he can't be just anybody, but a person of good reputation. It doesn't mean that he is perfect, but he must be known for his spiritual maturity. In other words, when describing his character, people don't identify him primarily or fundamentally with some negative characteristic. They don't say something like, "Oh, yes, I know Paul. He's the one who is always getting angry!"

2) *Husband of one wife*

Paul is not saying he has to be married. Otherwise he himself would not be living according to his own counsel! 1 Corinthians 7:7-9 suggests that Paul was not married. Some think that he would have to be married to be a member of the Sanhedrin, but others say that such a regulation was not in force until after Paul's time.[37] On the other hand, the text in Titus hints that it is normal for an elder to be married. Obviously it would not be correct to *forbid* elders to marry.

The point here is that he should not have more than one wife! If this requirement sounds a bit strange, remember that in New Testament times, monogamy was not as universal as it is today. Even among the Jews of that time, some accepted polygamy.

But there is another important application for us today. This points to something beyond the legal marriage situation. It calls for marital fidelity and sexual purity.

---

[37] Richard N. Longenecker, *The Ministry and Message of Paul* (Grand Rapids: Zondervan, 1971), 23-24.

3) *His children are believers and not open to the charge of debauchery or insubordination.*

Since only the Lord can convert someone, how can we require that an elder's children be believers? Is there another meaning for this phrase?

In the original Greek, the word translated "believers" is an adjective, *pistá*. It can be translated as "faithful" (See Matthew 25:21, 2 Timothy 2:2 and 2:11). It has a broader meaning, and does not necessarily mean that his children have been converted. The rest of the verse indicates that his children should not be rebellious, without discipline ("open to the charge of debauchery or insubordination"). Apparently he is making the same point as in 1 Timothy 3:4-5, that an elder should "govern his house well."

4) *A lover of good*

It is not enough just to behave well simply because it is your duty. A Christian should really want to do good and love what is good.

5) He must hold firm to the trustworthy word as taught.

This is the only specific mention of sound doctrine in this passage. It refers to the body of teaching of the apostles. A leader should not only believe sound Bible teaching, but "cling" to it. Note that according to Titus 1:9, a leader should correct those who oppose faithful teaching. One aspect of understanding the truth properly is knowing how to distinguish between truth and false teachings, and also how to defend the truth.

Our Leaders

Read 1 TIMOTHY 3:1-7.

What does verse 5 tell us about the function of an"overseer"?

What are the characteristics of an "overseer"? (or elder)

Again, some of these characteristics are clear, but others need explanation:

1) Sober-minded

The term in Greek literally means that he is not an alcoholic, but it also points more widely to the fact that he has self-control, he is serious, and has a clear mind. It does not mean that he never consumes alcoholic beverages, but that if he does, he uses them carefully and in moderation. To be serious does not mean that he never laughs or that he has no sense of humor, but that he can become serious when the situation demands it. He takes serious things seriously. He is a person that people can trust.

2) Able to teach

Up until now, all the characteristics of the elder that have been mentioned are attributes that every Christian should cultivate. It's just that a higher level of maturity is required in these areas on the part of the church officers. But the requirement "able to teach" is something especially for elders. Not all Christians have to develop this aptitude.

An elder does not need to be a seminary professor or a gifted public speaker. He just has to know how to share the teachings of Scripture in a way that helps others in their spiritual growth. He must have sufficient biblical and theological knowledge to avoid serious errors, and must have the ability to explain the teachings clearly. Not all elders can teach publicly in group settings, but they should at least know how to teach in personal conversations.

3) He must manage his own household well, with all dignity keeping his children submissive.

Paul emphasizes this characteristic by giving a brief defense of it. He says, "for if someone does not know how to manage his own household, how will he care for God's church?" (vs. 5) Church leaders should act as spiritual "fathers" for the members of the church. They should love them, teach them, encourage them, and sometimes correct them. A person who does not know how to love and discipline his own children will not be a good spiritual leader in the church.

4) Not a recent convert

The reason given in verse 6 is that a person who is a very new Christian might easily become arrogant about having a place of leadership. As the text continues, pride led to the fall of Satan, and as we know, it also led to the fall of man. Therefore, we should avoid situations that may encourage it.

How much time as a Christian is sufficient to become an elder? Paul does not stipulate any specific time, and therefore, each church will have to ask for wisdom to evaluate the candidates for themselves. However, my personal opinion is that it would be wise to wait at least two years after the person has made a profession of faith.

5) He must be well thought of by outsiders.

It is not enough for church members to have a good impression of the elders. They should also be respected by those who are not from the church. The idea is that sometimes it is easier for them to present a good image in Christian circles than in a non-Christian environment. For example, the work environment may cause temptation. If the others around them do not share Christian values or live according to the same ethical principles, those who are weak may begin to live inconsistently with their faith. That is why elders should also have a good testimony among the "outsiders" as well. It is there where you can really tell if a person is strong or not. To fall into the "snare of the devil" simply means to become entangled in sin.

Read ACTS 20:17 and 28.

To whom is Paul speaking in this passage?

What is the task of the elder according to verse 28?

Notice again that Paul calls the elders "overseers." The word here in Greek is also *epískopos*, just like in Titus 1:7, but this time in plural form. Again, this shows that Paul talks about "elder" and "bishop" as the same office, and not as two different offices. Paul is saying that elders are overseers.

Read 1 PETER 5:1-4.

What is the work of an elder, according to this passage?

Conclusion: The elder is a SPIRITUAL SUPERVISOR.

Normally, some of the key duties that the elders fulfill are the following:

- Meet regularly to discuss the plans, problems, and people of the church
- Supervise the selection of other church officers, including the pastor
- Supervise the training of other leaders
- Visit church members to care for them spiritually
- Lead home groups, teach Bible Studies, and teach Sunday School
- Help lead the worship service and the administration of the sacraments

REVIEW QUESTIONS

1. What is an "elder" ("presbyter")?

2. How was the term used in the Old Testament?

3. How are the terms "elder" and "bishop" related, according to Paul?

REFLECTION QUESTIONS

1. Is there any characteristic of an elder that you don't understand exactly?

2. What characteristics especially stand out to you?

3. Which of the characteristics are the ones where you feel you need to grow more?

(If you have a serious problem with any of them, please talk to your pastor o another leaders of your church.)

b. Pastor

Read 1 TIMOTHY 5:17-18.

What is the distinction that Paul makes between some elders and others?

Some make a distinction between the office of elder and the office of "pastor." However, instead of talking about a separate "office," it would be more in keeping with the New Testament to speak of elders that have special functions. As we explained above, an elder is a spiritual supervisor. And according to 1 Timothy 5:17-18, some of the elders dedicate more time to governing the church and also to preaching and teaching. Technically, the office is the same, but in practice, most churches need an elder who can work full time in the ministry, preaching, teaching, supervising the other elders, and supervising the church in general.

This elder is usually called a "pastor." In many Presbyterian churches, they call them "teaching elders," as opposed to the other "ruling elders." Usually, more preparation is required of the pastor, probably several years of study. This in itself justifies using another name for these men. Larger churches usually have several pastors, the "senior pastor" and maybe a "youth pastor," an "associate pastor," or an "executive pastor."

83

The Bible does not forbid such a practice, nor the use of the term "pastor." In fact, in the New Testament, we see that some elders took on positions of special leadership. James was an important leader in the Jerusalem church (Acts 15:12-21, 21:18). Peter and John were also leaders in Jerusalem (Acts 15:7, Galatians 1:18). None had the authority of what might be considered the first "pope," and the term "pastor" did not become a technical term for a different office in the New Testament, but some elders were respected and recognized as special leaders.

Read GALATIANS 2:9.

What does Paul call James, Peter, and John?

A pastor should be a "mentor," a "trainer." He shouldn't try to do everything himself, but learn to delegate responsibilities. He should train and encourage especially the other elders.

The name "pastor" is a good one, because it represents the spiritual care of the members of the congregation. It also reminds us of Jesus, who is the perfect example of a pastor. In their book, *Gospel Coach*, Scott Thomas and Tom Wood highlight four aspects of pastoral care: 1) The pastor knows his sheep. 2) The pastor feeds his sheep. 3) The pastor guides his sheep. 4) The pastor protects his sheep. [38]

Read JOHN 10:3-5.

How does a pastor guide his sheep?

---

[38] Scott Thomas and Tom Wood, *Gospel Coach* (Grand Rapids: Zondervan, 2012), 37.

Why do they follow him?

Read JOHN 10:14-16.

From what does the pastor protect his sheep?

How does Jesus show that he loves His sheep?

Read JOHN 21:15-17.

What did Jesus ask Peter three times?

What did He tell him to do three times?

Conclusion: A pastor is a PRINCIPAL SPIRITUAL SUPERVISOR.

REVIEW QUESTIONS

1. What is a pastor?

2. What is the difference between a pastor and an elder?

c. Deacon

The word "deacon" comes from the Greek Word *diákonos*, which means "servant," "helper," or "minister." It seems to be considered a separate office alongside the office of elder in passages like 1 Timothy 3:8-13 and Philippians 1:1. This term was not used in the Old Testament to speak of an office of leadership, and the office of deacon does not appear until the New Testament.[39]

While the term "deacon" is not used in Acts 6, some consider this to be the moment when the office was established. It is clear that the leaders recognized the need to diversify their labors and name qualified mature people to carry out a special kind of ministry. Furthermore, the manner in which they made a formal selection of these men, even laying hands on them, suggest that it was an official position.

Read ACTS 6:1-7.

What was the problem among the believers in Jerusalem? (v. 1)

What was the solution? (vs. 2-3)

What were the deacons to be like? (v. 3)

To what did the apostles dedicate themselves? (v. 4)

How were the deacons chosen? (vs. 5-6)

What was the impact of this solution in the ministry in Jerusalem? (v. 7)

The responsibilities of the deacons are related to administration, helping the needy, and managing material and financial affairs. Nevertheless, this does not mean that

---

[39] "Diácono" in *Diccionario Ilustrado de la Biblia*, Editorial Caribe, 165.

their ministry is not also a "spiritual" ministry, or that their activities never overlap with those of the elders.

Read ACTS 6:8-10 and 7:1-2.

Besides helping the widows, what did the deacon named Stephen do?

Read 1 TIMOTHY 3:8-13.

Are the characteristics of a deacon very different from those of the elders?
(Compare this passage with 1 Timothy 3:1-7.)

Although their work is normally supervised by the elders (the "overseers"), we should not consider this office as somehow inferior. The deacons have a different function, but it is also worthy of honor.

There are a few differences between the characteristics of deacons that are mentioned here and those that are mentioned for elders in 1 Timothy 3:1-7 and Titus 1:5-9, but not many significant differences. Notice that deacons are not necessarily expected to be "able to teach." Some other characteristics of elders are missing here, and a few new terms are mentioned (like "not double-tongued"), but there are not enough differences to suggest that the need for spiritual maturity is any different. For deacons, Paul says that they should be "tested" first (1 Timothy 3:10), but the requirement that an elder should not be a new Christian seems to point to something similar.

Verse 11 mentions women. In Greek the word is *gunaikas*, which can be translated either as "women" (as in the ASV and CEV) or as "wives" (as in the ESV and KJV). This has been interpreted three different ways: a) women who hold the office of deacon, b) women who do not hold the office of deacon but do diaconal work as helpers of the ordained men deacons, or c) as the wives of the deacons. Since it is inserted here within a passage dealing with men deacons (notice that verse 12 goes back to speaking of men deacons who should have only one wife), I am inclined to think Paul is speaking here of the wives of deacons. However, this does not mean that women cannot carry out diaconal ministries.

The subject of the role of women in the church is too much to deal with here, but I would suggest a few key points to consider. First, I believe that women are created equal to men in honor, that they have the same gifts that men have, and that their gifts should be used in our churches. However, just as in the family, men and women are equal in honor, but have been given different roles (Ephesians 5:22-33), the same applies to the church. Remember that even in the Trinity, while the Father, the Son and the Holy Spirit are equal in honor and glory, they have different roles.[40]

Read JOHN 13:14-15.

What did Jesus do to the disciples?

What was His purpose?

Every Christian should imitate Jesus in his service to others.

---

[40] For further reading on the biblical view of the role of women, see James B. Hurley, *Man and Woman in Biblical Perspective.* (Wipf and Stock, 2002, previously by Zondervan, 1981).

Read MATTHEW 23:11.

What can we learn about serving others in this verse?

If we follow the example of Acts 6, we should have deacons to relieve the elders from having too many responsibilities. They should avoid letting them get so involved in the physical and material affairs of the church that they can't carry on other key aspects of their ministry.

Some churches have leaders that carry out the functions of an elder, as seen previously, but they call them "deacons." While this can be confusing when you compare it with the New Testament language, it is not necessarily wrong to use that name differently. The important thing is not the terms we use, but making sure that the ministries of those whom the New Testament calls "elders" and "deacons" should both be included in the church. Furthermore, I think it is better to have two separate offices. If a church has only one office, and they expect these leaders to do everything that both elders and deacons were doing in the New Testament churches, they will probably have the same kind of problem that the church of Jerusalem had, as seen in Acts 6!

Read PHILIPIANS 1:1

Whom does Paul greet?

This text suggests that a distinction was made between the "overseers" or elders and the "deacons."

Conclusion: A deacon is a MINISTER ESPECIALLY DEDICATED TO THE PHYSICAL AND MATERIAL AFFAIRS OF THE CHURCH.

Some of the common duties of deacons are:

- Managing the finances of the church
- Taking care of the church building and properties
- Visiting the sick and elderly
- Planning and supervising social activities and fellowship activities of the church
- Counseling

REVIEW QUESTIONS

1. What situation in Acts 6 led to naming deacons?

2. What is the ministry of a deacon? Define his role.

REFLECTION QUESTIONS

1. Do you see yourself more as an elder, a pastor, or deacon? Why?

2. Does your church have a full time pastor? Does it have elders? Deacons? Explain what officers you have in your church and what they do.

3.2. Other Ministers

Read 1 CORINTHIANS 12:1-30.

What is the purpose of spiritual gifts? (vs. 7)

Who has these gifts? (vs. 7)

To what does Paul compare the Church?

What practical point does Paul make about our relationships by using this analogy?

Do you see any of your own gifts in this passage?

Read ROMANS 12:3-8.

Do you identify with any of the gifts mentioned in this passage? Which ones?

Read EPHESIANS 4:11-16.

What is the special ministry of pastors (shepherds) and teachers, according to this passage? (vs. 11-12)

What is the overall goal of the ministry? (v. 13)

According to verse 15, what are two key elements for helping the Church grow?

All Christians have spiritual gifts, and all Christians are "ministers" to help build the body of Christ, making it more like Him. Leaders should identify their own gifts and also help all the other members discover their gifts, then train them to minister to others.

It is not easy for everyone to identify their spiritual gifts. How do you know what they are? First, normally a person instinctively tends to do those things for which he or she is more gifted. That may already give you an idea. Also, I would recommend talking with the church leaders, and with friends and family, to see what gifts they find in you. Thirdly, you could test your gifts by carrying out ministry activities and evaluating the fruit you see from those experiences. Remember that a person usually has a mixture of gifts. You might look for web sites that offer free online tests to help discover your gifts.

Also, instead of trying to identify specific gifts mentioned in the passages we just looked at, it might be helpful to think about the seven different areas of ministry that we explained previously. Take another look at the figure of the cross and try to identify the areas where you consider yourself most gifted and most inclined to participate.

THE MINISTRY

1. Worship
2. Prayer

7. Fellowship

6. Service

5. Evangelism

3. Teaching
4. Sacraments

These distinctions are not an excuse for avoiding other areas of ministry. Someone might say, for example, "I don't have the gift of evangelism," to justify his passivity. We *all* should do *all* ministries at *some* time and in *some* way. Rather, the distinctions are meant to help us know where we should give greater emphasis.

In later chapters, we will discuss different aspects of the ministry, giving practical suggestions on how to carry them out.

REVIEW QUESTIONS

1. What is the purpose of spiritual gifts?

2. Who has spiritual gifts?

3. Who should be considered "ministers" in the Church?

4. What is the special task of the teachers and pastors?

5. What is the overall goal of the spiritual growth of the Church?

REFLECTION QUESTIONS

1. Have you been able to identify some of your spiritual gifts? What are they?

2. Are you able to identify your most important areas of ministry? What are they?

3.3. The Call and Preparation of Leaders

Read 1 TIMOTHY 3:1.

Is it good to desire to be a leader? Why?

Read ACTS 20:28.

Who places leaders in the Church?

Read ACTS 6:1-7.

Explain the process of selecting the deacons. How were they chosen, and how were they officially designated as deacons?

Notice that the selection process involved the people of the congregation, but it was supervised by the apostles. Notice also that they prayed and laid hands on them. This act symbolizes the confirmation that God has called them.

Let's look at a few examples of key leaders in the Bible, to see how God prepared them.

MOSES

Read EXODUS 2:11-12.

What did Moses do?

If you only knew what you observe in this incident, would you consider this kind of person a good candidate for a leadership position in your church?

Read EXODUS 3:1-4:17.

What excuses did Moses give to avoid accepting God's call to go to Egypt?

What do you think Moses' real problem was in resisting the call?

How did God answer him?

What does this passage teach us about the insecurity to accept God's call to some kind of ministry? What is the solution?

What does this passage teach us about the kind of person that God can use as a leader in the ministry and about how He prepares them?

JEREMIAH

Read JEREMIAH 1:1-10.

What excuses did Jeremiah give to avoid accepting the call?

What do you think Jeremiah's problem was in accepting the call?

How did God answer him?

What did the Lord do to him? (v. 9)

What does this passage teach us about the kind of person God calls to the ministry?

What does it teach us about how the Lord prepares people for ministry?

There was once a conversation between the Wesley brothers, John and Charles. One of them was a famous preacher and the other was a famous composer. One said to the other, "If God gave me wings, I could fly." The other replied, "If God asks me to fly, I know he will give me the wings." This second attitude is the one we should cultivate. If God calls you to be a leader, He will give you everything you need to carry out the ministry!

If we think about it, we can see that many of the men used by God did not necessarily demonstrate outstanding human talent. If God always used very talented people, they would possibly receive the glory and not God.

We can also see that many of the leaders that God used have had serious ethical and spiritual problems. However, the Lord transformed them and used them. It makes it abundantly clear that it is only by the grace of God that someone can become a leader. Only the Lord calls us and only the Lord enables us.

Obviously this does not mean spiritual maturity doesn't matter. Nor does it mean that we should try to show how sinful we are so that God can receive more glory when He call us to leadership!

> What shall we say then? Are we to continue in sin that grace may abound? By no means! How can we who died to sin still live in it?
> **ROMANS 6:1-2**

But it does mean that you should be encouraged if you feel a little uncertain of your abilities or your level of spiritual maturity. Look to the Lord and trust in Him! He will enable you! We should avoid the two extremes of either being discouraged by our weaknesses on the one hand, or being passive and taking our weaknesses too lightly on the other hand.

PETER

Read JOHN 18:15-18 and 25-27.

What did Peter do?

Read JOHN 21:15-19.

What did Jesus ask Peter three times?

What do you think? Why did he ask him three times?

What did Jesus tell Peter to do three times?

Do you believe that Jesus forgave Peter?

What can we learn from the example of Peter about how God prepares leaders?

REVIEW QUESTIONS

1. Who calls a leader to serve in the Church?

2. What can we learn from the examples of Moses, Jeremiah, and Peter about how God calls and prepares leaders?

REFLECTION QUESTIONS

1. Do you sometimes feel uncertain of your call to be a leader in the ministry? Why? Do the examples of Moses, Jeremiah, and Peter encourage you?

2. What would you think if you are not sure of your call to leadership, but the current leaders and the members of the congregation ask you to do it and approve you?

3. What would you think if it were the other way around? That is, what if you consider yourself a leader, but the congregation does not agree?

3.4. High Expectations

A pastor in Chile decided to take a survey in his church, to see what his members expected of him as a pastor. He told me later that the results indicated that they wanted their pastor to be Jesus himself!

I recently attended the installation of a new pastor, where another pastor warned that members would ask him to go to all church meetings, to have time to listen to all their problems, to eat at all their homes, to play sports with them, and much more. He said, "You can do all that, but you'll be dead in three months!"

Some members are what we call "high maintenance" people, demanding constant attention. Steve Brown once commented that he had resigned as a pastor because he was "tired of being the mother to so many people."

The problem is that the leaders fall into a trap: they want to please everyone. This quickly develops a kind of co-dependency, in which the leader needs to be needed, and he has a hard time saying no.

This applies to spiritual things as well. Many expect leaders to be spiritual giants. Again, the problem is that the leaders easily try to project the spirituality that people expect of them. This leads to a facade of false spiritual maturity.

People have unfair expectations of the children of leaders too. Some people don't allow them to be normal children. Other children may run around in the church, but the pastor's children can't. Other children may talk during service, but the leaders' children can't. This is especially unfair, because when the leaders are at church, it is just the context in which they need to give time to other people, leaving them less time with their own children. The result is that people see their children at their worst. The saddest thing is that these unfair expectations tend to produce a rebellious attitude on the part of the children of the leaders.

What can we learn from the following passages about the proper attitude of a leader?

MATTHEW 6:1-4

ROMANS 12:3

2 CORINTHIANS 12:7-10

REVIEW QUESTIONS

1. What are some of the high expectations that the people have of their leaders?

2. What is the trap into which leaders often fall when they feel that there are very high expectations of them?

REFLECTION QUESTIONS

1. Have you ever felt the pressure of unrealistically high expectations? In what way? How did it affect you?

2. What can we do to manage unfairly high expectations?

Chapter 4: Our Integrity; in Heart and Mind

Human excellence,
apart from God,
is like the fabled flower which,
according to the Rabbis,
Eve plucked when passing out of Paradise.
Severed from its native root,
it is only the touching memorial of a lost Eden--
sad while charming and beautiful,
but dead. [41]

Sir Charles Villiers Stanford

In one of the novels of C.S. Lewis, young Eustace has become a dragon, because he has done something wrong. Then Aslan the lion (a figure of Jesus) removes the layers of scales, little by little. It hurts, but in the end he is happy to be a young man again. That's the way it is in our spiritual life; It hurts when the Lord begins to take away the ugly aspects, but it is good for us, and in the end, we are happier.

The theme of this chapter is "integrity", focusing especially on the heart and the mind of leaders. We will look deeper to see where we need a special work of the Holy Spirit. Our most serious problems are below the surface, and we have become accustomed to avoid thinking about them. We will examine the war of desires, how we manage our

---

[41] Quoted by Steve Brown in *A Scandalous Freedom* (New York: Howard Books, 2004), p. 51.

fears, the problem of perfectionism, and our very way of thinking.

This chapter, as well as the following chapter on relationships, can also serve as a guide for discipling members of your church. Every Christian needs help in the areas of integrity and relationships!

Read PROVERBS 4:23.

What should we keep with all vigilance?

Why?

Read ROMANS 12:2.

What needs to be renewed so that we can be transformed?

We need to care for both our heart and our mind. Before beginning this reflection and self-evaluation, remember that we will not grow spiritually by simply trying to be better. Our desire is not to make you feel guilty, or to lead you to focus too much on yourself, trusting your own efforts to grow spiritually. As Steve Brown says, "The greatest cause for our not getting better is our obsession with not getting better." He adds, "Holiness hardly ever becomes a reality until we care more about Jesus than about holiness." [42]

---

[42] Steve Brown, *A Scandalous Freedom*, 53.

4.1. The Heart of the Leader

Any self-effort to overcome sin and sanctify ourselves will only lead to failure. As the quotation by Stanford at the beginning of the chapter says, if it does not come from the Lord, it will be like a flower without roots, dead. (This story of the flower that Eve took from Paradise is not in the Bible. As it says, it is a "fable." Here we use this quote simply as an analogy to make a point.)

However, part of the process of spiritual growth involves examining ourselves in the light of Scripture. It is like evangelization; If a person doesn't hear the law, he won't know his sin or his need for Christ. In a similar way, if we don't see what God asks of the leaders of His Church, we won't understand the great need we have to depend totally on Christ for our growth.

There is a story of some spies who were captured during the Second World War. Their captors tried to make them confess by using psychological manipulation. They discovered problems and mistakes they had made in their lives, and confronted them to make them feel guilty. All but one finally collapsed emotionally and signed the confession. How did the other one resist? When they confronted him with his mistakes, he always answered something like, "Oh, that's nothing! You don't know half of what I've done! I'm much worse than you think!" This teaches us something important: for our own mental and spiritual healing, we need to acknowledge our sin, confess it, and accept the Lord's forgiveness.

Read PSALM 51.

In what particular sin was David possibly thinking when he composed this psalm?

What were some of the deeper things that he confessed?

Read ROMANS 7:19-20.

What are the deeper things that Paul confesses here?

a. The War of Desires

JAMES 4:1 says:

> What causes quarrels and what causes fights among you? Is it not this, that your passions are at war within you?

Note the language of war. The word translated "passions" is *hedonón*, which means desires, pleasures, or lusts. The word translated "at war" is *strateuoménon*, which means to fight or wage war, like a soldier. The phrase translated in the ESV as "within you" is a translation of the Greek phrase which means literally "in your members" (*en tois melesin humon*). The ASV translates it more literally, "... your pleasures that war in your members." The KJV says, "...your lusts that war in your members." Normally the word "members" is related to the body, either literally or in a figurative sense.

The context of this verse has to do with conflicts among *people* in the church. The point is that the members of the body, the local church, are in conflict because their personal desires are selfish. However, I believe that the verse can also be applied to the conflict of desires that exists within the heart of each individual. Any temptation we face can be understood as a "war" of desires. In a moment of temptation, we have both good desires and bad desires in conflict.

For example, suppose my doctor tells me that I should minimize the amount of sweet foods that I'm consuming, because it is bad for my health. Then I go home, open the refrigerator, and see in front of me a beautiful chocolate cake! At that moment, the desire to eat the cake is a bad desire. At other times, in another situation, or for other people, it may not be a problem, but for me at that moment it is. However, I have another desire that is good, the desire to take care of my health. In my heart there is a "war of desires." This is what happens to Christians whenever we face a temptation.

Sometimes it seems that our bad desires have the victory over our good desires. With certain sins, we may even feel that we will never win the battle. However, the Bible says that Christians will have victory.

Read ROMANS 6:14.

It says that sin will not have _____ over us.

Let's consider how we can overcome strong temptations. In a sense, any sin can become an "addiction," something that enslaves us. Some of the same steps that help alcoholics or drug addicts can also help every Christian in his struggle with sin.

Read ROMANS 7:15-23.

What does Paul recognize with respect to the power of sin?

Read PSALM 32:1-4.

What happens when we deny our sin?

What happens when we confess it?

Read 2 CORINTHIANS 1:9 y 2 CORINTHIANS 12.7-10.

Why is it important to admit our weaknesses?

Read ROMANS 7:24-25.

Where do we find victory over sin?

Read 1 JOHN 1.9.

What does the Lord do when we confess our sin?

How much does He cleanse?

Jesus went to the cross in our place, and suffered the punishment we deserved. From the cross, he shouted, "My God, my God, why have you forsaken me ?!" (Matthew 27:46). At that time, He was paying for our guilt.

Jesus the Reservoir

The heart of Christ became like a reservoir

in the midst of the mountains.
All the tributary streams of iniquity,
and every drop of the sins of his people,
ran down and gathered into one vast lake,
deep as hell and shoreless as eternity.
All these met, as it were, in Christ's heart,
and he endured them all.

(Charles Spurgeon, 1859)

Read EPHESIANS 4:22-32.

What figure is used here to explain spiritual growth?

It's difficult to stop a bad habit, without replacing it with a good one. Analyze your most difficult struggle, the sin that especially leads to addiction, and think about what should replace it. Ask the Lord for forgiveness, and ask for His help to replace the bad with the good.

Write down what you can do to replace the sin that is causing you problems.

Instead of looking only at sins and evil desires, we must look more at the good that should replace sin, focus on good desires, and focus on Christ Himself. One of the keys to winning the war of desires is to strengthen good desires. By contemplating the good things and the beauty of Christ, sin will not be so attractive anymore!

Read PHILIPPIANS 4:8.

Write down the things we should think about.

107

REVIEW QUESTIONS

1. We need integrity in our _____ and in our _____.

2. What is the error we should avoid when we think of our sanctification? What is the author's warning?

3. What is the analogy of Sir Charles Villiers Stanford about making an effort to grow and sanctify yourself spiritually?

4. According to James 4: 1, what war do we fight?

5. What is the key to winning this war?

REFLECTION QUESTIONS

1. What is one of the wars of desires that you have to fight frequently? What is the bad desire? What is the good desire? How can you win this war?

2. Think of some sin that tends to be a struggle for you, something that you tend to repeat, something that is difficult for you to overcome. Write your sin on a piece of paper, ask for forgiveness, then tear it up and throw it away, symbolizing the Lord's forgiveness. Now write down something you can do to replace the sin, a good habit to replace the bad habit. Ask the Lord to heal you.

b. Managing Our Fears

David Seamands, in *Healing Grace*,[43] explains that no one receives totally unconditional love from their parents and close relatives. Because of this absence, we begin to seek love in the wrong way: a) some try to succeed, b) others try to please, and c) still others try to control things to avoid suffering. The downside of this situation is that we always live with the fear of not having done enough. As a result, a) some are afraid of failure, b) others are afraid of rejection, and c) others are afraid of losing control. These fears affect our behavior more than we realize.

All this comes from the Fall that affected our own heart and our relationships with others. After Adam and Eve sinned, the Lord called Adam and asked him where he was. Adam responds, "I heard the sound of you in the garden, and I was *afraid*, because I was naked, and I hid myself" (Genesis 3:9-10).

Fear manifests itself in many ways, and has multiple consequences. Seamonds explains some of them. Whatever our past may be, we are now responsible for the way we react. It does not help to simply get angry with our parents. With the Lord's help, we can overcome these fears and their effects.

Read 1 JOHN 4:18.

What is the result of understanding God's love?

---

[43] David A. Seamands, *Healing Grace* (Wheaton, IL: Victor Books, 1989), 87-106.

To overcome our fears, it helps to remember that the Lord loves us unconditionally. What we have not received from our family and our friends, the Lord Himself provides. He satisfies the need for acceptance, love, and security. We no longer have to try to achieve success, to please others, or to control things.

Read PHILIPPIANS 3:4-9.

What does Paul think of the "success" he has achieved?

Why?

What is true "success"?

Read ROMANS 8:1.

How does this verse affect your sense of being "accepted"?

Read ROMANS 8:14-15.

What is our relationship with God now?

Read ROMANS 8:28-31.

Why don't we need to be "accepted" by other people?

Why don't we need to control things?

Ask the Holy Spirit to do a very deep work in your heart, making significant changes far below the surface, in areas you don't even understand. Give your heart and your life totally to the Lord.

Remember that in this life we will never fully overcome sin. Don't let discouragement overwhelm you and make you give up. Live each day and every moment depending on the Lord.

For some reason the Lord made us in a way that we need to sleep every night. Think of each day as a new beginning, as a "resurrection." Keep your sight always on Jesus, and do not look so much at yourself.

REVIEW QUESTIONS

1. What are the three fears mentioned in this section?

2. According to 1 John 4:18, what overcomes fear?

3. To overcome our fears, what things should we remember?

REFLECTION QUESTIONS

1. In which of the three ways mentioned by Seamands do you tend to seek love?

2. Do you sometimes experience the fear related to that area?

3. How does this fear affect you?

4. Did the points made in this section help you in any way? How?

c. The Problem of Perfectionism

When I applied to be a missionary with my denomination, one of the steps in the evaluation process was an interview with a Christian counselor. I will never forget the conversation. He said I was fine, but that I had a problem with perfectionism. I began to reflect on this, and I had to admit that I still had not overcome the legalism I had developed since my childhood. Over many years now since the interview, I have been thinking more about grace as I study the Bible, reading more books about grace, and talking with people about grace. Now I consider this one of the most important areas of my spiritual pilgrimage. Although I still struggle with legalism and perfectionism, I think the Lord has been working on me in this area.

Perfectionism is an attempt to control your own sanctification, demanding too much of yourself. The result is that you waver between a sense of guilt and a feeling of superiority.

One of the first books that helped me was *The Cost of Discipleship* by Dietrich Bonhoeffer, a Lutheran Pastor from Germany. In the introduction, there is a quote by the author, in which he says that we should stop trying to make something out of ourselves, even if it is to become a saint, and that we should "throw ourselves into the arms of God."[44] Apparently, this comes from another book, *Letters and Papers from Prison*. These are his reflections when he was in prison for participating in the resistance against Adolf Hitler, where he died shortly before the end of the war.

---

[44] Dietrich Bonhoeffer, *The Cost of Discipleship* (New York: Macmillan, 1975), 24.

This comment helped me, because I was striving to be good, and it made me realize that, although it may not seem like it on the surface, this is actually self-centered. He reminds us that Jesus teaches us to *die* to ourselves. If we are always thinking about our own spiritual state, we are still focused on ourselves, instead of really dying to ourselves. Our attention should be on Christ, not on ourselves.

How can we avoid this ego-centric focus? It seems impossible, because if I'm thinking about how I can change MY focus, I'm still thinking about ME! Bonhoeffer's response is that we must "throw ourselves into the arms of God." It's the only way!

Another thing that helped me was the story of Martin Luther and the Bible passage that transformed him. Luther also struggled with perfectionism. He punished himself to make himself more holy, he fasted and prayed, but could not find peace with God. Then he read Romans 1:17 in a different way.

Read ROMANS 1:17.

What do we need to obtain righteousness?

From where does righteousness come?

What does it mean that the righteousness of God is revealed "from faith for faith" (or "from faith to faith" as in the KJV)? In the Greek, it says, *"ek pisteos eis pistin."* The word "ek" is a preposition often used to indicate movement from the inside out, for example when someone leaves a house. The second term, "eis," is used to indicate movement from the outside to the inside, for example when someone enters the house. Literally then, it says that justice comes out

113

of faith and goes into faith, or begins in faith and ends in faith. I believe the NIV translation communicates the idea: "by faith from beginning to end." The Christian life is like a bridge; we begin by faith on one side, and we end by faith on the other side. The pillars that hold up the bridge on both ends is the grace of God, and we receive that grace by faith.

This verse is an introduction to the whole letter to the Romans, which first deals with the theme of justification (chapters 1-5) and then deals with the subject of sanctification (chapters 6-8). What Paul indicates in the introduction is that our righteousness does not come from us, but from God, and that we receive it by faith. Then in the letter, he shows that our righteousness includes both our justification and our sanctification. This is very important, because some people think they are justified by faith upon conversion, but that they have to continue their Christian life of sanctification by self-effort. To avoid perfectionism and legalism, it is essential to understand that sanctification is also by faith.

C. S. Lewis also speaks of the results of perfectionism, as well as the solution:

> For, make no mistake: if you are really going to try to meet all the demands made on the natural self, it will not have enough left over to live on. The more you obey your conscience, the more your conscience will demand of you. And your natural self, which is being starved and hampered and worried at every turn, will only get angrier and angrier. In the end, you will either give up trying to be good, or else become one of those people who, as they say "live for others" but always in a discontented grumbling way -- always wondering why the others do not notice it more and

always making a martyr of yourself. And once you have become that, you will be a far greater pest to anyone who has to live with you than you would have been if you had remained frankly selfish.

The Christian life is different: harder and easier. Christ says, "Give me ALL.... Hand over the whole natural self, all the desires which you think innocent as well as the ones you think wicked -- the whole outfit. I will give you a new self instead. In fact, I will give you Myself: my own will shall become yours."[45]

Read ROMANS 7:21-25.

What does Paul recognize in terms of his ability to overcome sin?

What is his conclusion? Where does he find help?

Read 2 CORINTHIANS 3:16-18.

According to this passage, how can we become more like Christ?

Read HEBREWS 12:1-2.

What lessons can we learn from these verses about the Christian life?

Are we passive in the Christian life?

---

[45] C. S. Lewis, *Mere Christianity* (New York: Harper, 1980), 196-197.

However, as we run, where should we fix our attention?

Why? What does this mean?

It's difficult to understand how to harmonize the sovereignty of God with the responsibility of man, but this analogy of the race helps a lot. When people ask what my favorite passage in the Bible is, I say Hebrews 12:1-2. It's important to me, because it helps me overcome legalism, without leading me to irresponsible passivity. The passage teaches us that we should keep running, but always looking to Christ for strength. We can do nothing without Him. He is the author of our faith and He continues to perfect our faith.

Finally, Steve Brown is another author who has helped me deal with perfectionism and self-effort. In one of his books, he tells an illustration of a child who wanted to learn to play the piano. The teacher began to give him lessons, and gave him the assignment to learn "Twinkle, Twinkle, Little Star." When the child tried to show him what he had learned, he wasn't doing very well. But the teacher reached his arms around the child, and helped him to play it. He explained that he was always going to help him, and that he would always turn his efforts into something wonderful. I love the story, because it shows that we are not passive, but when we take a step of faith, the Lord takes our weak attempts, puts His arms around us, and makes a beautiful melody![46]

REVIEW QUESTIONS

1. What is perfectionism? What's the result?

---

[46] Steve Brown, *When Being Good Isn't Good Enough* (Thomas Nelson, 1990), chapter 2.

2. What does Bonhoeffer say about trying to make something of yourself? What should we do instead of fixing our attention on ourselves?

3. What does Romans 1:17 teach us about righteousness?

4. What does C. S. Lewis say about perfectionism?

5. What does Paul recognize in Romans 7 about his ability to overcome sin?

5. What does Hebrews 12:1-2 teach us about the Christian life?

REFLECTION QUESTIONS

1. Do you sometimes struggle with perfectionism? How does it affect you?

2. Do the biblical passages in this section help you avoid perfectionism? Explain how.

4.2. The Mind of the Leader

Sometimes we evangelicals suffer from what I call "intellectual schizophrenia." By that I am not talking about mental illness, but rather that when we speak of certain topics we consider "spiritual," like the sovereignty of God for example, our main source is the Bible, but when we talk about other subjects such as science, art, politics or economics, our main source is something we have read in other books or what we have seen on television. We need to learn to integrate our faith better with every field of thought, going back to the foundation of the Bible to orient our thinking.

Read ROMANS 12:2 again.

How can we avoid being conformed to the world?

Read 2 CORINTHIANS 10:5.

What should we do with every thought?

Read EPHESIANS 6:14.

What is the first piece of armor that we should put on?

Note the following points regarding a biblical concept of truth:

1) We depend totally on God for the truth.

Read PROVERBS 1:7.

What is the beginning of knowledge?

When I was in college, I began to doubt everything I had been taught in the church and in my home, even the existence of God. Then the Lord showed me one night when I was looking at the stars that He was really there, and I surrendered my life to Him. Soon I encountered people who made me doubt the Bible. While living with this uncertainty, I realized that if I didn't believe the Bible, I couldn't really be sure about *anything!* I wanted to believe it, but could not justify it in my own mind.

I went to seminary, not because I felt a call to be a pastor or missionary, but because I was looking for answers. Thankfully, I had the privilege of taking classes with Cornelius Van Til, who I consider one of the greatest apologists of the twentieth century. It was his exposition of the story of Adam and Eve that convicted me of my problem. He explained that, when God told them they would die if they ate from the Tree of the Knowledge of Good and Evil, they responded in an illegitimate way. As they questioned, "I wonder...., I wonder.... who is right?", they were arrogantly pretending to be able to find the truth by themselves, independent of God. In fact, they were setting themselves as judges over God Himself, their very creator. Van Til says that this is man's basic problem in seeking the truth. After all, who are we to question Him who has made us?

When I read this, it pierced my heart. I realized I was doing the very same thing when I questioned God's Word in the Scriptures. I was putting myself over God as judge. I asked Him to forgive me and I finally stopped doubting. God became my source of all truth. I thought, "If God says the moon is made out of green cheese, then I will change my idea of the moon and of the color green and of cheese! If God says it, it's true!" Of course, God will never make a statement that so clearly contradicts our normal use of language, reason, and observation, but this idea expressed my new attitude of absolute submission to His Word.

The biblical concept of truth is God-centered. It recognizes that God is the source, the author, the origin, of all truth. Then God, knowing ALL, being the very SOURCE of truth, decided in His mercy to reveal to us something of the truth. Therefore, we can be sure of what He tells us. We are part of His creation, and we must submit to Him. We need to recognize our absolute dependence on Him, even in our thoughts. The result of this submission is certainty of knowledge. It's the only way to be sure of something.

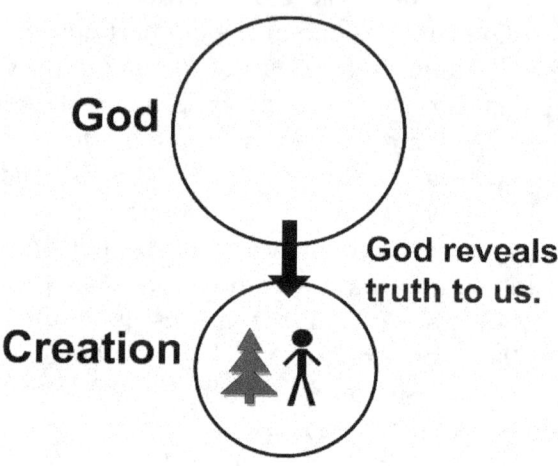

God

God reveals truth to us.

Creation

2) The Bible is our main source of truth.

God reveals some of His truth in creation and in history, but it is important to emphasize that His main instrument for revealing truth is His written Word, the Bible. The Holy Spirit uses especially the Scriptures to teach us and help us grow.

Read JOHN 17:17.

What is the truth?

How does it benefit us?

Read JOHN 14:26.

Who will teach us?

What will He teach us?

Read TITUS 2:1.

What does Paul tell Titus that he should teach?

One aspect of forming a Christian mind is to understand sound theology.

3) The truth should be lived.

We tend to think of the truth as something purely intellectual. We think that we "know" the truth if our mental concepts somehow correspond to objective reality. But biblically speaking, we are not really knowing the truth in the complete sense of the word, unless we are also living it. For example, we might say we know that God loves us and that He works all things together for our good. However, in a moment of unnecessary anxiety, are we really "knowing" those truths?

Read 2 TIMOTHY 3:16-17.

For what are the Scriptures useful?

What is the purpose?

Read JOHN 8:31-32.

In what are we to remain as disciples of Jesus?

What will be the result?

You can see two things from this passage: First, knowing the truth is not just an intellectual exercise, but rather it is part of a disciple's trusting relationship with his Lord. Knowing the truth means being faithful to God. Secondly, if we really know the truth, it will change our lives and make us free.

REVIEW QUESTIONS

1. In what sense do evangelicals sometimes suffer from "intellectual schizophrenia"?

2. What is the first piece of armor mentioned by Paul in Ephesians 6:14?

3. To know the truth, we depend totally on _____.

4. What is God's main instrument for revealing His truth?

5. To really know the truth in a complete biblical sense, we must also do what?

REFLECTION QUESTION

1. Do you agree with the Christian concept of truth that was presented in this section? Why?

2. Do you think you are trying to submit to the Lord every area of your thinking? What can you do to "take captive your thoughts to Christ" in a more consistent way?

Recommended Additional Reading

Brown, Steve. *A Scandalous Freedom* (New York: Howard Books, 2004).

Brown, Steve. *When Being Good Isn't Good Enough* (Thomas Nelson, 1990).

Ramsay, Richard. *Intellectual Integrity*. (http://www.lulu.com/spotlight/rbramsay)

Seamands, David A. *Healing Grace* (Wheaton, IL: Victor Books, 1989).

Wolfe, Richard. *Character of Christian Leadership*. (http://www.lulu.com/shop/richard-wolfe/character-of-christian-leadership/paperback/product-22809961.html)

Chapter 5: Our Relationships; Keeping Priorities

God is more interested in you
and your personal relationship with Him
than a thousand lifetimes of good works.[47]

Dr. Charles Stanley

Of course God is interested in our ministry and in our actions. If we love Him we will keep His commandments (John 14:15). But sometimes we make the mistake of turning this around; we think if we are doing good things, then we are obviously loving the Lord. However, our relationship with God is more than keeping the commandments out of a sense of duty. The same principle applies to all our relationships.

One of the greatest dangers of the ministry is that, when a leader begins to spend too much time in ministry activities, he forgets to care for his personal relationships. If you make this mistake, everything else starts to fall apart! Rev. Peter Scazerro was the pastor of a rapidly growing church in New York City. But a conflict arose among the pastors that produced a division in the church. Scazerro became anxious, giving more and more time to the ministry, desperate and in a bad mood, trying to solve all the problems. He didn't realize that this was leading him to neglect his own family. After his

---

[47] Charles Stanley. "The Priority of Relationship," "In Touch Ministries," August 1, 2017.
<https://www.intouch.org/read/magazine/daily-devotions/the-priority-of-relationship>

wife attempted many times to encourage him to rest more and give more time to his family, she finally told him that she would no longer participate in their church! She and the children began to attend another worship service! Obviously this startled him, so he found help and began to change his priorities. He began to give more time to his family, to take a real day of rest every week, and to take vacations from time to time.[48]

Our priorities are relationships: with our spouse, with our children, with the members of the church, and above all, with the Lord.

Read 1 CORINTHIANS 12:31-13:3.

What is the most important thing? Why? In what sense?

We can summarize the results of the Fall in terms of our relationships. Sin produced conflicts between man and God, between man and woman (and all other human beings), between man and nature, and between man and his own heart.

---

[48] Peter Scazzero, *The Emotionally Healthy Church* (Grand Rapids: Zondervan, 2003), 20-36.

And we can also summarize the results of salvation in terms of the restoration of these relationships.

Read EPHESIANS 1:7-10.

What does this passage teach us about the meaning of salvation?

What does it teach us about the importance of relationships?

We can use the analogy of a garden to talk about our interpersonal relationships. The garden concept teaches us many things, especially that, in the same way that we need to take care of the plants in a garden but cannot control the results, we also have to be faithful in our efforts to maintain good relationships, but we do not control the results.

Read 1 CORINTHIANS 3:6.

Who planted?

Who watered?

Who caused the growth?

This point is important, because it helps us avoid becoming anxious, feeling unduly guilty when there are problems, and being proud when things are going well. The Lord asks us to be faithful, but only He gives the fruit.

5.1. Our Relationship with Our Spouse

The wife of an elder, a deacon, or other church leader is in a difficult situation. Many times she operates behind the scenes, serving almost invisibly, without much recognition. When the church members admire her husband, they often forget that she is always there supporting him. But if someone has a conflict with her husband, she has to be careful not to get involved, and she has to put up with problems without saying anything. The same might occur with the husband of a woman who has a leadership role.

Therefore, the leader should make a special effort to encourage his or her spouse, and to maintain a good relationship.

What can we learn from the following passages?

1 PETER 3:7

EPHESIANS 5:25-28

The main sources of conflict in a marriage are:

- poor communication
- lack of intimacy
- differences about managing money
- differences regarding how they raise their children
- unfaithfulness
- differences regarding their sexual relations, and
- false expectations

Christians sometimes argue about what love is for a couple. Is it a feeling? Is it a commitment? Is it a decision? In some Eastern cultures, parents arrange marriages, and often this turns out fine. However, in the Western world, we want to fall in love before getting married. Which is best?

The illustration of a plant can help us develop a balanced Christian view of love in the context of marriage.

Think of the different aspects of a couples' relationship:

a. The roots represent Christian faith.
b. The branches represent friendship.
c. The leaves represent wholesome interests and activities outside the marriage relationship.
d. The flowers represent the romantic aspect of marriage.

a. Christian Faith (the roots)

This is the main source of nourishment. Without these roots, it is difficult to maintain a healthy marriage.

Read 2 CORINTHIANS 6:14.

The phrase "unequally yoked" (*heterozugeo* in Greek) means "differently united." It could communicate the idea of two different types of animals connected to the same yoke, but it could also convey the idea of two animals of the same type connected in a different way, perhaps one tighter than the other, or one straight and the other crooked. In any case, this unequal connection makes it difficult to cooperate and pull the weight properly. One might be pulling harder than the other, or maybe they would even be pulling in different directions.

The Bible tells Christians to marry a person who is also a Christian. Otherwise, they will not share the same values, the same beliefs, or the same purpose. I am so grateful that Angelica and I can talk about almost anything, and even thought we may not always agree, we know there is a common base of a Christian worldview. Furthermore, in every marriage there are conflicts, and without a common faith, it is difficult to overcome them. Without the Holy Spirit, we would not have the supernatural power to love one another and to resolve conflicts. (This does not mean that if a Christian is currently married to a person who is not a Christian, that he should get a divorce and remarry a Christian. See 1 Corinthians 7:12-13.)

It's important to pray together, share the Word, share Christian books, Christian songs, and to encourage each other. Each family is different, and we do not have to share in the same way. When I was a child, our family had a regular time to read the Bible and pray together. But for me, sometimes it seemed a bit forced and mechanical. Therefore, with our own family, when our children were still at home with us, Angelica and I tried to avoid making it a routine. Sometimes we would read something and pray, but not always. Sometimes we would just talk spontaneously. But it is good to do *something* to share and encourage one another spiritually. In the last few years, now that our children are grown, the two of us usually read a few pages of a good Christian book after breakfast (Angelica likes to read out loud), and then we pray together. This nourishes our relationship at the roots.

b. Friendship (the branches)

The branches are more visible than the roots, but of course depend on them.

Read GENESIS 2:18-25.

According to this passage, what is the purpose of marriage?

Angelica is my best friend. She is my partner, my greatest support. When I'm not with her, I feel I'm missing something. I really enjoy talking with her, and we talk about everything: people, places, theology, literature, music, movies, politics, economics, languages, everything! Since communication is key to any friendship, especially marriage, we should make time to talk, to really talk.

It's important to understand our differences; we have to learn to "translate" what each other means. Angelica and I come from different countries and different cultural backgrounds. When we were children, we spoke different languages. However, I always say that the most important differences we have are the differences between men and women, even more than our cultural differences.

Women are more complex, as seen in the humorous illustration below. According to the picture, the man has one single switch: on or off. The woman, on the other hand, has many switches and many dials, which can be adjusted in many ways. It's an exaggeration, but the main point is valid.

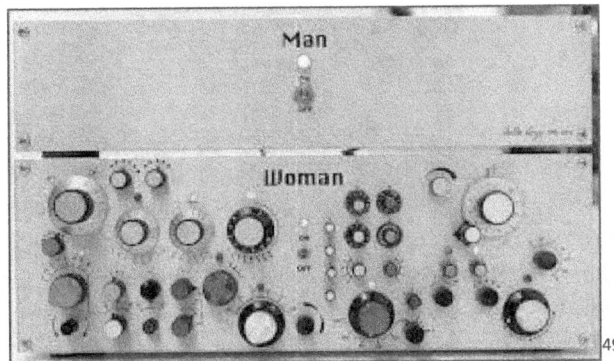

We also have to learn to "listen" to non-verbal language (the major part of communication!) Women are more subtle than men in expressing some things.

When a woman shares a struggle she is having, she often is not necessarily asking us to give her solutions, but would appreciate our understanding and concern. She probably already knows what the solution is.

Some authors speak of different "love languages."[50] We need to know what the primary love language of our spouse is and communicate with her in that language. According to the observations of some, we can distinguish the following ways in which people sense love most easily:

1) physical touch
2) words of affirmation
3) quality time

[49] <http://etherealmind.com/humour-men-vs-women-machine-knobs/> Nov. 17, 2016.

[50] Gary Chapman, *The 5 Love Languages* (Grand Rapids: Zondervan, 2015).

4) receiving gifts
5) acts of service

You may have other observations or other ways to explain our differences, but these categories help me understand my own family. Angelica thinks it's easy to say a few words, but in order to feel loved, she needs to see actions. She also enjoys spending time in conversation. Nicolas, our son, likes to spend time together, watching sports, playing the guitar, or listening to music. Melany, our daughter, appreciates words of encouragement and a hug. I also respond best to words of affirmation. It's important to clarify that the point of this is not for me to insist that others understand *my* language, but for me to learn to speak the language of *others*, especially my wife! Also, remember that people may change over time.

It's essential that we learn to resolve conflicts, forgiving each other and showing grace to each other.

Read JOHN 13:1-15.

Notice that Jesus kneeled down to wash the disciples' feet. When Peter resisted, he said, "If I do not wash you, you have no share with me." He also said that they were all clean except for one. Obviously in this context, washing symbolizes forgiveness. The passage teaches us that we should serve one another, as Jesus served the disciples, but I believe that the main application is that we should *forgive* one another as Jesus forgave us. Forgiveness is an act of service; we do it by grace, not because the person who has offended us deserves it.

If it's hard for me to forgive someone, it's probably because I'm in the wrong position in the scene. I am probably sitting in the chair, waiting for the one who offended me to serve me, to ask me to forgive him. But according to the passage, if someone has offended me, I should let *him* sit in the chair, and I should kneel down and wash *his* feet and forgive him.

When it's hard for me to forgive someone, I ask myself if I think I am superior to that person. The answer is always yes. But the moment I remember that I am not really superior, I can forgive him. We are all sinners deserving condemnation. Compared with our holy loving God, none of us can claim spiritual superiority.

Once I felt very hurt by a group of people, and it was difficult to overcome the feeling of anger. One day I was praying in a church room, and looked at a painting of a flock of sheep following a shepherd. I thought to myself, "That's what they are! They're a bunch of stupid sheep!" Immediately I had to ask myself just where I belonged in that picture. Obviously I was not the pastor, who was a figure of Jesus! I realized, "I guess the only option is that I'm another stupid sheep!" At that moment, the Lord changed my attitude, and I was able to forgive the people who had offended me. We can apply these same principles to our marriage.

c. Wholesome Interests and Activities Outside the Marriage Relationship (the leaves)

The leaves are another source of nutrition for plants. In the process of photosynthesis, the leaves receive energy from the sun and transform it into food for the plant and into oxygen. This is a figure of what we need in marriage: another source of energy and nutrition.

Both spouses need other activities outside of marriage. This provides things to talk about, and avoids boredom. It prevents one from totally depending on the other for his social life and his well-being. Former US president Jimmy Carter once said that when he retired, it was the most difficult period of his marriage. The two felt trapped in the house together, with no other outside activities, and they almost got divorced!

This is especially important for women who work at home. But it is also good for the man to have time with his friends. It is good to have a hobby, like a sport, or some musical activity.

d. The Romantic Aspect of Marriage (the flowers)

The romantic aspect of marriage, including sexual relations and intimacy in general, is also important. Feelings can live and die, like flowers on a plant, but they are beautiful! For this aspect to function well, the roots, the branches, and the leaves need to be healthy first. But it is still a healthy and essential aspect of marriage.

While men often complain that they want more sexual activity than the women, women often complain that they want more romanticism. How long has it been since you bought flowers for your wife, or some other gift? Do you often give her a loving hug and express words of appreciation?

We are very selfish, more than we realize! Curiously, I have learned that even singing a song to my wife can be selfish. Once I noticed Angelica was a little discouraged, and decided to sing her a song, while playing the guitar to accompany it. Meanwhile, I was thinking to myself, "What a good husband I am!" "Look what I'm doing to encourage her!" And to be honest, I thought it sounded pretty good! But on this occasion, for some reason, it didn't seem to help much. Suddenly I realized that I was thinking more about myself than about her! Selfishness is so deep and deceptive that we often don't see it. Finally I started thinking more about her came up with another idea: let *her* sing a song! When she selected one of her favorite songs and began to sing, only then did I notice a positive change. It is not always easy, but we need to learn to put ourselves in the place of our spouse.

Romantic feelings can't be forced, but they can be encouraged. The Lord has made us in such a way that, by thinking of the other person and showing her affection, the romantic feeling grows and produces a mutually positive effect. A hug is a good illustration. When I give a hug to Angelica, who am I thinking about? About her or about me? If I only thought of the pleasure it gives me, it would be inappropriate and selfish. However, if I'm thinking first about her, it also becomes pleasing to me! If I seek my own happiness in marriage, neither one of us is happy. But if I seek first the good of my spouse, it brings joy to both of us!

Conclusion

To keep a good marriage, remember the garden principle: There are things we should do, but we can't control the results. Only God controls the results.

A few years ago, Angelica and I visited "Giverny," the garden of the famous artist Monet, near Paris. It has a pond with a small green bridge that appears in one of his most famous paintings. It's a beautiful place, with all kinds of flowers and plants, a small stream that runs through it, and pathways for walking. As we strolled through the garden, I thought about how extraordinarily clean everything was, and I noticed there were no weeds or insects. First, I thought it had to do with the place, the weather, or the soil, but then I saw the gardeners! I counted nine men who spent their whole time pulling up weeds and taking care of the plants! No wonder the garden was so clean! Remember that the Lord is the best gardener! He is the one who takes care of the garden of our marriage and our family!

REVIEW QUESTIONS

1. The priorities in our lives should be our _____.

2. What are the four relationships that we must take special care to maintain?

3. If marriage is like a plant, what are the parts, and what does each part represent? Mention the lessons we can learn from each part of the plant.

4. What are the major causes of conflict in marriages?

5. What are the five "love languages" mentioned in this section?

REFLECTION QUESTIONS

1. What are the major causes of tension in your own marriage?

2. What do you do as a couple, or as a family, to share a time of spiritual nourishment?

3. What is your spouse's favorite "love language"? How can you express love in that language?

4. Do you and your spouse have wholesome interests and activities outside of your marriage relationship? What are they?

5.2. Our Relationship with Our Children

A friend once told my wife how difficult it was for him to be a pastor's son when he was young. Wanting to be hospitable to visitors, their parents sometimes neglected their own children. For example, when someone would arrive late at night unexpectedly, sometimes he had to get up and leave his bed to make room for the visitor. Years of this kind of experience produced resentment.

We heard from another son of a pastor who left the church and denied the faith, saying that "he could not love a God who took away his parents." Obviously, he was not a priority for his parents. Pastors, elders, deacons, and other church leaders sometimes make the mistake of giving more time to the ministry than to their own children.

Like plants, our children need care, time, attention, and spiritual nourishment; if we don't give it to them, they can dry up, have weak roots, or stop producing flowers. Our children should be a higher priority than visitors, church members, or work.

If we think they don't really care how much time we give them, we are very wrong. An important man wrote in his diary one day, "Today, I went fishing with my son. A day wasted!" The boy wrote in his diary the same day, "Went fishing with my father today -- the greatest day of my life!"[51]

Regarding discipline, I think that the tendency of society has been to not discipline enough, to not set proper limits. I have seen parents in a store who first say "no, no, no" when their child insists that they buy him something, but when the child keeps crying and shouting, they finally give him what he wants. With that, they are teaching the child exactly how he should behave to get what he wants: cry and scream! After a few years of this game, the child will have serious problems. I will never forget a counseling session I observed when I was in seminary. Some parents were seeking help because they had problems with their daughter. When the counselor let the daughter speak, her complaint was not exactly what the parents expected; she said, "They have never told me no! They always let me do what I want!" The parents couldn't believe it. They thought they had been loving her by always giving in to her wishes.

Children, especially when they are young, need limits to feel safe and secure. An experiment was made in which they

---

[51] Josh McDowell, *The Father Connection* (Nashville: B&H Publishing, 1996), 74.

first took some small children to a playground without fences. In this case, the children tended to stay close to the teacher and not explore the surroundings. Then they took the same children to another playground with fences that clearly defined the play area. Here they played more freely and explored all over the area. Apparently they were more afraid without the fences, and they felt more free and safe when they had clearly defined limits.[52]

Read PROVERBS 13:24.

If we love our children, what will we do?

However, sometimes evangelicals go to the other extreme, being too authoritarian and too strict, without taking into account their ages or personalities. Instead of caring also for their children's hearts, they focus only on making sure they respect their authority and obey, even when they are older. Some go too far with physical punishment. I know some families who have punished their children so much that they have rebelled against God. I know other families where adolescent children do not dare talk at the table, or if they talk, they always look at their parents to see if they approve of what they are saying. They don't really feel free to express their own opinion. We need a balance of showing unconditional love and providing adequate limits with appropriate discipline.

Read EPHESIANS 6:4 y COLOSSIANS 3:21.

---

[52] American Society of Landscape Architects, August 4, 2017, <https://www.asla.org/awards/2006/studentawards/282.html>

What error should we avoid?

I'll never forget a conversation I had with a psychiatrist in Chile. He told me he was an atheist, but that he had nothing against Christianity. However, he told me that many of his patients were evangelicals, and that he wanted to give me some advice. He told me that he observed a lot of negativity in our churches that caused a lot of unnecessary guilt. He told me that we should talk more about positive things, like God's love. I think he was right. We need to put more emphasis on the grace of God in general, and this also applies to the way we deal with our children.

We don't have to correct everything. Sometimes it's better to lose a small battle in order to win the war. When our children were teenagers, sometimes we had conflicts over how messy they left their bedrooms. But when this started to cause a lot of serious tension between them and us, we decided that it was better to stop insisting so much on that, in order to avoid greater problems. There are more important things. You may not agree with me, but looking back, I think it was the right decision.

Every child is different. When our son Nicolas was a baby, I could easily calm him down if he was crying. I would sit him on my knee and bounce him up and down. It was a magic remedy; it never failed. However, with Melany who was born two years later, for some reason, the same treatment just didn't work. When they were students, they had different ways of studying and different interests. Nicolas liked mathematics and science, while Melany preferred literature and philosophy. They have different personalities and different ways of relating to people.

Therefore, we have to treat each child differently. I am not saying that we have different norms for their behavior, but the way we try to achieve the desired behavior may be different. Possibly a more authoritative or more direct method will work with one, but not with the other. Some tend to be more submissive by nature, while others are more strong-willed.

Some parents think they know exactly how others should raise their children. But no one knows their children as well as their own parents. There are biblical guidelines that are for everyone, but how to apply them can vary. Don't let a person whose children are in another stage of life than yours, or whose children have different personalities than yours, tell you how to raise your own children.

Like plants, children also go through different stages of growth. When they are small children, they need to learn to obey, and to respect the authority of their parents. They need more rules and more discipline. However, when they are teenagers, we have to start preparing them to be independent. We need to think more about their hearts, their own values. The question is, how will they be when they are no longer at home with us? Will they make the right decisions without our help? Will they have the right values and principles in their own hearts? Adolescence is a stage in which we need to talk more, to listen more, to instill values and principles. Finally, when they are adults, we don't give them authoritative instructions as we did before. Someone said that when our children are adults, the general guideline for our role is to "influence, not to give instructions." We have to let them take responsibility for themselves. In the stage we now live, with our children as adults, it helps me to think of grammar; avoid verbs in the imperative mood!

Although it is not the main point of the passage, I think we can apply the teaching of Galatians 3 and 4 to raising our children.

Read GALATIANS 3:23-4:7.

In this passage, Paul makes an analogy: God's people were more like a child during the Old Testament, and now they are more like an adult. The relationship with the law has changed. God's people were more like a "slave" then, but now they are like an adult son. This means greater freedom, but also greater responsibility.

In a similar way, our adult children have a different relationship with us now. When they were little, we had to say, "Don't touch the stove!" or "Don't cross the street!" Now we say, "Take care of yourself!" We trust they have the maturity to know how to apply the principle themselves. Again, this means more freedom, but it also means greater responsibility. They will have to be accountable to the Lord for their own decisions.

Read LUKE 18:16.

What are we told to do in this passage?

Our most important task as parents is to bring our children to the Lord. This doesn't mean just taking them to church, or just praying and reading the Bible with them. Nor does it mean that we can convert them. It means doing what we can to help them develop their own relationship with Him.

Read DEUTERONOMY 6:4-9, 20-25.

In what moments should we talk with our children about spiritual things?

We need to be authentic. Nothing pushes our children away from the Lord more than our hypocrisy. It's not necessary to share every ugly detail of the struggles we have with sin, but we should be transparent. Dr. Jack Miller always projected a closeness with the Lord, and often spoke of the need to repent of sin. I think the farthest thing from his mind was to make people think he was holy. However, when his daughter Barbara was a teenager, she rebelled and was dragged into the world of drugs. Years later, the Lord changed her heart and she became a Christian. The two of them wrote a book about their experiences, called "Come Back, Barbara!" In this book, they take turns writing about their experiences. She writes what she was living in a certain period of time, and he writes how he saw everything at the same time. What is striking is that Barbara struggled with her father's image as a very spiritual person. She saw in him on a spiritual level that was simply impossible for her to achieve. So she decided that she could never be like him, and rebelled, surrendering to sin. Her father never imagined what she was feeling in her heart.[53]

Their story teaches us again that we can't control the results of raising our children, much less their conversion. Only God can change their hearts and give them faith. We have friends who are excellent parents, but their children are not believers. Some have problems with addictions. Other children come from very dysfunctional families, but turn out well, by the grace of God. Like plants, we need to do our best to take care of them, but we don't determine exactly what they will be like.

---

[53] C. John Miller and Barbara Miller Juliana, *Come Back, Barbara* (Phillipsburg, NJ: P&R Publishing, 1988).

A Lesson from the Farm

Our relationship with our children has a great influence on their relationship with God. My dad disciplined us when necessary, but we always knew that he loved us. He played with us and taught us important things. I have great memories of him laughing and joking, but I also remember that he was fairly reserved and sometimes seemed a bit serious. He was the principal of an elementary school, but he also had some land that he had inherited, a field in which we cultivated wheat.

We helped him off and on during the year, plowing, planting, and maintaining the machinery, but my favorite time was the summer harvest, when we saw the fruit of our labor. My job was to drive a truck. I had to wait in the field, watching carefully, ready to go immediately to get the wheat when I saw it piling high in the bin of the combine (the harvester machine), and then when the truck was full, to drive the load to town. One day I saw the heap of wheat visible above the combine that my dad was operating, and I knew I had to move quickly. He didn't like to wait; it could rain, it could hail, or a tornado could come, and we could lose the whole crop. In my haste, I crossed over the field without realizing that I was driving right through some thick mud. The truck stopped, and the wheels began to spin uselessly. I turned off the engine and got out to see how serious it was, and found that the wheels were buried a foot deep!

But the worst thing was that I saw my father coming with the combine, driving slowly across the field. He had started far away, and it seemed like it was taking forever! When he was finally getting close, I didn't want to see his face. I grabbed a shovel and started frantically digging mud from around the wheels. I knew it was useless, but I wanted to show him that at least I was doing something. The combine stopped close by, ...and I kept digging, ...and digging, ...but I couldn't look up. "He must be furious!" I thought. He didn't move, and eventually I had to look. However, when I dared to see at his face.... I saw he was smiling! Not laughing at me, but just smiling kindly. I couldn't believe it! For some reason, he wasn't angry.

I had obviously exaggerated the seriousness of the crisis, and more importantly, I had distorted the character and personality of my father, underestimating his love and understanding. He simply hooked up a chain and pulled the truck out of the mud. I will never forget that day, because I felt the love and acceptance of my father. He taught me something about God that day, more than he could ever explain in a hundred conversations; he taught me about the grace of God. And it was a perfect illustration of the gospel: we are stuck in the mud of sin, but God loves us, forgives us, and pulls us out of the pit.

We teach our children about God, but we ARE NOT God! The most important thing is to help them develop their own relationship directly with the Lord.

Read JOHN 15:4-5.

What is necessary to bear fruit?

Our children need to be "connected" directly to the Vine, which is Jesus Christ. Let's pray that the Lord touch their hearts, that they may have sincere personal faith in Him, that they may grow in their faith, and bear fruit!

REVIEW QUESTIONS

1. What is the tendency of society regarding the discipline of children?

2. What problem sometimes exists in evangelical families regarding the discipline of children?

3. What is the balance we need in our relationship with our children? What extremes should we avoid?

4. Explain how the relationship with our children changes during the different stages of their lives.

5. Nothing distances the children from the Lord more than _____.

6. What did the author learn about God from his father, when he got stuck in the mud on the farm?

REFLECTION QUESTIONS

1. What are the biggest difficulties you have had with your children?

2. How did your relationship with your parents affect your relationship with God?

3. What suggestions do you have about parenting?

5.3. Our Relationships with Church Members

I would like to offer some brief suggestions for maintaining good relationships with local church members, whether you an elder, a deacon, pastor, or any other leader. Of course, biblical guidelines for relationships in general also apply to leaders. We must love everyone and manifest the fruit of the Spirit in all relationships. Note what the following passages teach us about our relationships with church members.

1 CORINTHIANS 13:4-7

GALATIANS 5:22-23

What aspects of love and the fruit of the Spirit do you especially need to demonstrate more?

There are also some special guidelines for leaders.

Read 1 PETER 5:1-3.

What do we learn from this passage?

Sometimes a position of leadership produces an attitude of superiority or a tendency to abuse authority. Some may think of the church as they would a business organization, and since they have been appointed to be a leader, they think they have the right to tell others what to do. Obviously this passage says that it shouldn't be that way.

A distinction is often made between being aggressive, passive, or assertive. Being aggressive means not showing respect to others. Being passive means not asking others to show you respect. Being assertive means respecting others, but also asking them to show you respect. What we should strive for is to be assertive.

If you are waiting in line at a bank, and someone tries to crowd in front of you, how do you react? This situation will reveal whether you are acting in a passive, aggressive, or assertive manner. A passive person will not say anything and let the person crowd in. He may be angry, but he says nothing. An aggressive person will insult the offender and force him to go back to the end of the line where he belongs, without showing respect. An assertive person would talk to the person first. The person crowding in may have a real emergency. He may have been in line before, and just left for a moment. Or maybe he is with another person who was keeping his place for him. If there is some good explanation, then you can just let it go. But if the person was crowding for no valid reason, then the assertive person can kindly ask him to go back to his proper place. If it's hard for you to speak up in such a situation, it might help you think about all the other people behind you in line. It's unfair to all of them. You can also think about the person who is crowding; if you don't say anything, it only encourages him to continue being a disrespectful person. Usually, if you speak kindly and respectfully, the person reacts properly and goes back to the end of the line. Of course it's not worth starting a fight over something so insignificant, but you can try to be assertive.

Church leaders can't do everything that people ask of them, nor can they always help in the exact moment that people want.

Read JOHN 11:6, 21.

What can we learn from this example of Jesus?

150

Remember that the principal role of a leader is to train others, "... to equip the saints for the work of the ministry, for building up the body of Christ" (Ephesians 4:11-12). No leader has all the spiritual gifts, or unlimited time. Leaders should dedicate themselves to train and supervise other members, to help everyone discover and use their own gifts. You shouldn't feel guilty when you can't do everything that people expect of you.

A good leader should be careful not to show favoritism. It's not that he can't have friends in the congregation, but he shouldn't have an exclusive group that he always spends most of his time with, while neglecting others. It is especially important not to show prejudice against the poorest or least educated, for example. He must love all and minister to all.

Leaders shouldn't pretend to be super-spiritual.

Read 1 TIMOTHY 1:15.

Read ROMANS 7:19.

What does Paul say about himself?

Leaders should practice the biblical guidelines for resolving conflicts.

Read MATTHEW 18:15-22.

If someone in the church offends another brother, what is the first step that must be taken to resolve the conflict?

What is the second step?

What is the third step?

How often should we forgive someone who has offended us?

Instead of telling gossip or just keeping grudges, we should seek reconciliation, first by talking to the person who has offended us alone. If this does not result in reconciliation, we should go with one or two witnesses. If that doesn't work either, we should approach the church officers to help resolve the conflict. In any case, we must learn to forgive.

Nevertheless, we have to be careful about conflictive people. We can't let them divide the church.

Read TITUS 3:10-11.

Read ROMANS 16:17.

How should we treat a person who causes division in the church?

REVIEW QUESTIONS

1. What are the general guidelines for having good relationships with church members, according to 1 Corinthians 13:4-7 and Galatians 5:22-23?

2. According to 1 Peter 5:1-3, what should leaders avoid in their dealings with members of the church?

3. What does it mean to be assertive? How is being assertive different from being aggressive or passive?

4. What are the steps we should take when someone has offended us, according to Matthew 18:15-22?

REFLECTION QUESTIONS

1. What do you consider the major causes of conflicts among church members?

2. Do you have any other advice on how to have good relationships with church members?

3. To what extent should we speak of our own sins in front of the congregation?

4. How can we practice both Matthew 18 and Titus 3:10-11?

5.4. Our Relationship with the Lord

This is our most important relationship! If we are not right with the Lord, we will not be well with anyone! We are talking here about our daily personal relationship with Him. One of the most dangerous traps of the ministry is to spend so much time working that we neglect our personal relationship with God.

Read PROVERBS 4:23.

What does this verse tell us about our priorities?

Read PSALM 42:1-2.

What is the psalmist struggling with? What can we learn from this?

In what ways can you seek the Lord's presence?

Many authors highlight three aspects of our spiritual well-being. Some speak of "mind, hands, and heart" (doctrine, action, and feelings). Dr. Richard L. Pratt, Jr., president of *Thirdmill*, makes the same distinction by speaking of the need for "orthodoxy, orthopraxis, and orthopathos." We should have the right thoughts, the right behavior, and the right feelings. He warns that in many evangelical circles the most forgotten aspect is "orthopathos".[54]

Steve Brown asks, "Have you ever been hugged by a doctrine?" Of course, sound doctrine is very important, especially for ministers and church leaders (Titus 2:1). But in his comical way, Brown highlights the fact that it is not enough to have the right doctrine; we also need love and a personal relationship with Jesus.[55]

D. Martyn Lloyd-Jones says:

> As theology is ultimately the knowledge of God, the more theology I know, the more it should drive me to seek to know God. Not to know about Him, but to

---

[54] See the video lessons from "Building Your Theology" <http://thirdmill.org/> .

[55] Steve Brown, *A Scandalous Freedom,* 161.

know Him. The whole object of salvation is to bring me to a knowledge of God.[56]

Things that impede a close relationship with God

Read ISAIAH 59:2.

What separates us from God?

Read JAMES 4:6-8.

What keeps us far from God?

Read 1 JOHN 1:8-9.

What removes the barrier of sin between us and God?

Pretending we have no sin only puts more barriers between us and the Lord.

Read PSALM 32:1-5.

How does the psalmist feel when he is not confessing his sin?

Legalism also impedes our relationship with God.

Read GALATIANS 3:1-3.

What was the error of the Galatians?

---

[56] <http://www.reformationtheology.com/2006/04/hows_your_prayer_life_by_dr_ma.php> Nov. 16, 2016.

By whose power are we sanctified?

Read ACTS 13:43.

In what should we continue? What does that mean?

Read ROMANS 1:16-17.

From where does righteousness come?

Then how do we obtain righteousness?

Why does legalism keep us away from the Lord? Because a legalistic attitude makes us look at ourselves and the law to overcome sin, instead of looking at the Lord and trusting Him.

Helps for drawing closer to God

God has given us some ways to keep close to Him. We call them the "means of grace."

Read ACTS 2:46-47.

Note the means of grace they were using.

Spiritual disciplines and the use of the means of grace are tools to maintain this relationship: prayer, the Word, the sacraments, and Christian fellowship.

However, the means of grace should not become mechanical. They do not achieve spiritual growth or closeness with God by themselves, but only as we trust Him to work in our hearts. That's why we call them means of *grace*. Unfortunately, it is possible to do all the right things with the wrong attitude.

Think of how God included rest times in the commandments and in the religious calendar of Israel. There is a day of rest, there is a year of rest, and a year of Jubilee. The purpose of these times of rest was especially to renew their spiritual life, their personal relationship with the Lord.

My experience is that I go through stages in the way I experience personal closeness with the Lord, and frankly I go through low periods and high periods. Sometimes it helps to focus on Bible reading and write down my thoughts in a spiritual diary. At other times, this becomes too mechanical, and for a change, I dedicate myself more to prayer. Sometimes a list of requests helps me pray, but it is usually better for me to just relax and meditate. I usually have a special place in the house where I sense the presence of the Lord, but that place can change. I also like to go for a walk in the evening, looking at the stars. I sense His presence by looking at nature: the stars, the sea, the mountains, the plants, or the clouds. Music also brings me closer to the Lord. Just like all people have different ways of relating better and communicating better, each Christian has his own way of drawing close to his heavenly Father.

Read HEBREWS 12:1-2.

Where should we look as we run the race of the Christian life? Why?

REVIEW QUESTIONS

1. What is our most important relationship?

2. What things tend to keep us from being close to the Lord? What should we do to eliminate them?

3. What are the means of grace that we can use to keep closer the Lord?

4. What is the error we need to avoid when using the means of grace?

5. What does Hebrews 12:1-2 teach us about the Christian life?

REFLECTION QUESTIONS

1. What do you do to keep close to the Lord?

2. What suggestions do you have?

Chapter 6: Our Ministry Activities; Part 1

Mafalda:
(as she jumps off the swing)

"As always;
as soon as you put
your feet on the ground
the fun stops!" [57]

Now we're going get off the swing and "put our feet on the ground," but hopefully it will not stop the fun! We have spoken of the heart and the mind of church leaders. Now let's talk about our "hands." We will look at some practical suggestions about the activities we do in our local churches. The activities are divided into two lessons. You may prefer to focus especially on the areas where you consider you have the strongest gifts, but it would be good to at least look over all areas of ministry, since a leader needs to be familiar with all of them.

Read 1 PETER 4:10-11.

In verse 11, Peter mentions two categories of ministry. What are they?

---

[57] Mafalda is a comic strip character produced by Quino (Joaquín Salvador Lavado), ed. Esteban Busquets. *10 Años con Mafalda* (México, D.F.: Penguin Random House Grupo Editorial, 2015), 43.

("Whoever _____, ...; whoever _____, ...")

Some people divide spiritual gifts and ministry activities into *Word* ministries and *service* ministries. While we can't make strict divisions between these categories, the distinction is helpful. For example, teaching, evangelism, the supervision of the worship services, and the administration of the sacraments are more directly related to the teaching of the Word. They require greater capacity for teaching and greater discernment of sound doctrine. On the other hand, prayer, service, and fellowship are more related to helping people in other ways. They require greater compassion and hospitality.

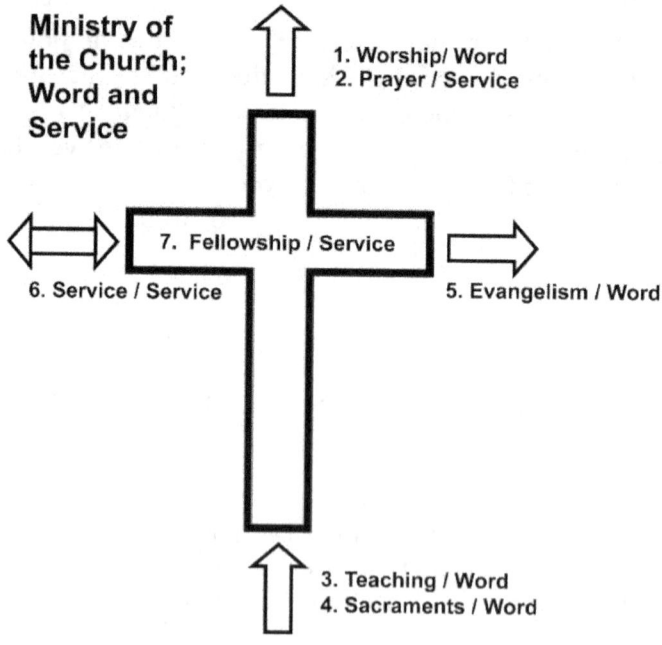

Ministry of the Church; Word and Service

1. Worship/ Word
2. Prayer / Service

7. Fellowship / Service

6. Service / Service

5. Evangelism / Word

3. Teaching / Word
4. Sacraments / Word

If we think of the differences between the offices of elder and deacon, we could also make a distinction between Word-related ministries and service-related ministries for them. The elders have more responsibility regarding the ministry of the Word, and the deacons are dedicated more to service. This does not mean that they are the only ones doing these activities, but that they would be the main supervisors. Following that scheme, we could roughly divide the ministries of the church into areas that would be supervised either by the elders or by the deacons.

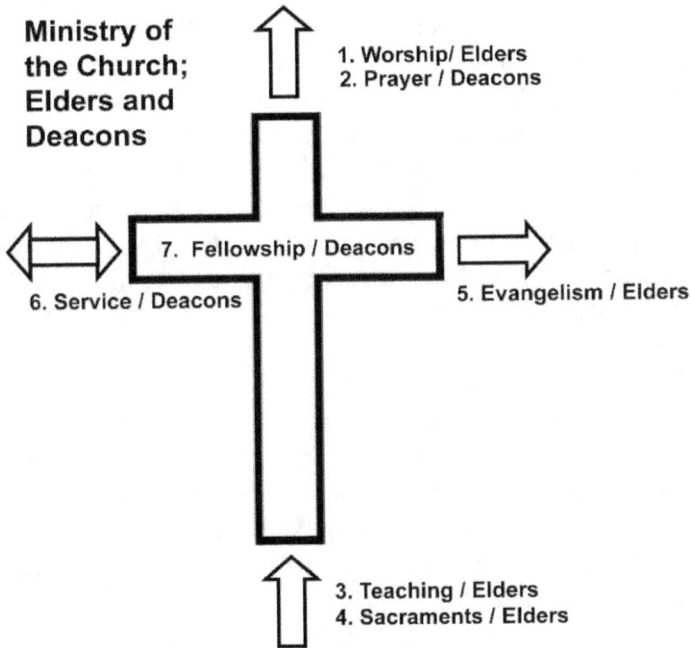

Ministry of the Church; Elders and Deacons

1. Worship/ Elders
2. Prayer / Deacons

7. Fellowship / Deacons

6. Service / Deacons

5. Evangelism / Elders

3. Teaching / Elders
4. Sacraments / Elders

In this chapter, we will look at the first four aspects of ministry: worship, prayer, teaching and the sacraments.

6.1. Worship

I would suggest the following guidelines for planning and directing a worship service:

1) The Main Purpose

The word "worship" comes from the word *proskunéo* in Greek, which literally means to fall down and kiss someone's feet in reverence. This shows the attitude of worship. To bow down before someone manifests honor and submission. Kissing their feet indicates love and gratitude. When we gather in worship, we are saying to the Lord, "We love you and honor you!"

It is easy to confuse the purpose of the worship service. Sometimes we think mostly about what we get from worship: what we learn from the message, the songs we like, and the joy we feel from seeing our friends, for example. So if we do not like the music, or if the pastor begins to preach sermons that do not mean so much to us personally, it is tempting to stop attending.

The worship service is a meeting of God's people with Him. Just as in marriage there are intimate moments when the two talk and share, so we Christians have special moments to meet with the Lord and tell him that we love him. The worship service is the most important activity of the week. We gather to pray, confess our sins, praise the Lord, and hear His Word.

When I fell in love with Angelica, I wanted to tell her she was beautiful. It was something I simply had to say! It was an instinct that I could not deny. It should be something like this with the Lord. The desire to praise him naturally arises from the fact of knowing him. The best way to prepare for worship is simply to get closer to the Lord and know Him better.

The one who directs worship must be concerned with helping the people sense the presence of the Lord. He should maintain an atmosphere of seriousness, but without losing the joy. The leader should be aware of how the people are feeling and try to lead them into an attitude of worship.

2) Two Essential Factors

Read JOHN 4:24.

How should we worship God?

These are the two essential factors in worship. To worship in spirit means to worship with the heart, with sincerity, guided by the Holy Spirit. To worship in truth means to worship with the mind, with right concepts, based on the Word of God. On the one hand, it is not enough to sing a hymn that has good lyrics, if we do not feel it in the heart. On the other hand, it is not right to sing a song with all the enthusiasm in the world, if the words are not biblical. Our praise must be both sincere and based on the Word.

One of the sacred responsibilities of pastors and church elders is to supervise what they are going to do in the worship service, so that it is worthy to present to God. They should check the words of the music, the selection of the songs, give suggestions for the prayers and any other aspect of the service. Some churches have worship directors or music directors, but even so, pastors and elders should supervise them. In general, we should look for guidelines in the Bible. We can't offer anything mediocre to God!

3) The "Regulative Principle" of Worship

The *Westminster Confession of Faith* says:

But the acceptable way of worshiping the true God is instituted by himself, and so limited by his own revealed will, that he may not be worshiped according to the imaginations and devices of men, or the suggestions of Satan, under any visible representation, or any other way not prescribed in the Holy Scripture. (Chapter 21, paragraph 1)

Some people have drawn from this paragraph what they call the "regulative principle" of worship. The main point is that our worship should be guided by the Word of God, not by our own ideas or desires. This should be obvious. After all, we are expressing our worship of the Lord, and therefore we want to do it *as He desires*.

The previous chapter about Christian liberty is also helpful. The point of the second paragraph is that we should respect freedom of conscience in general, and in a special way in matters of "faith" and "worship."

God alone is Lord of the conscience, and hath left it free from the doctrines and commandments of men, which are, in anything, contrary to his Word; or beside it, in matters of faith, or worship. (Chapter 20, paragraph 2)

Note the distinction between the commandments "contrary" to the Word of God and the commandments "beside it." In general, we must defend our freedom from commandments "contrary" to the Word, in whatever field. Even civil authorities, even our parents, even our leaders, cannot force us to do anything against the Bible. If our parents ask us to lie, we must refuse to do so. If our boss tells us to steal, we must resist. This is clear, and is especially seen in the case of the apostles, when the authorities forbade them to teach in the name of Jesus (Acts 4: 18-20). They explained that they had to obey God first.

However, if the authorities tell us to do something that is not *contrary* to the Word of God, but "beside it," normally we should obey. Here we should apply the principle of submitting to authorities (Romans 13:1). For example, they say that we must respect traffic signals, and that we should not exceed the speed limit. It's true that the Bible doesn't mention these specific commandments, but they are not "contrary" to the Word, and therefore we should obey.

Now let's look at the matters of "faith" and "worship." This principle is different. Here the Confession of Faith says that we have freedom from commandments related to these two areas, even when the commandments may be only "beside" the Word. For example, if the pastor teaches that we should believe that Jesus ate fish every day as a child, we do not have to believe it. It is a teaching "beside" the Bible, because the Bible neither affirms it nor denies it. If the pastor tells all men to wear a tie when they attend worship, we do not have to obey such a command. The Bible does not command it, but it does not prohibit it. Therefore, it is "beside" the Bible and we have freedom. You may choose to go along with this in order to cooperate and keep peace, but you are not obligated biblically.

The *Westminster Confession of Faith* was written in the context of the Reformation, when they were struggling with the impositions of the Roman Catholic Church. Because of the Catholic doctrine of Tradition, they insisted on some doctrines and practices that are not in the Bible. For example, they established the doctrine that Mary, the mother of Jesus, did not die, but ascended to heaven. They also had guidelines for worship services. The reformers wanted to maintain their freedom of conscience. They didn't want to be forced to *believe* anything "beside" the Bible, and they did not want to be forced to *do* anything "beside" the Bible *in worship*.

The "regulatory principle" and the principle of "Christian liberty" do not resolve all issues regarding worship, but they are helpful guidelines. We should plan the worship services carefully, making sure that our activities have biblical support, and that they do not *impose* anything "beside" the Word of God.

4) The Style of Music

What should the music be like?
Are different styles allowed?
How can we prevent this issue from dividing the church?

The style of music in worship is often a source of conflict. Some prefer a more contemporary style, and others prefer a more traditional style. In a church in Chile, we tried to introduce newer songs, songs composed by Latin American authors, but a very respected member of the congregation opposed it. When a group would sing more modern songs, with guitars and other instruments, he would sit on the front pew and look at them with a face of disapproval. But I have also heard contemporary songs that simply do not have good lyrics or good music, or songs in which the lyrics do not go well with the music. For example, there is a song with excellent lyrics about God's holiness, but the music is too light and playful for such a serious subject. I just can't sing it! There is another song with very solemn music, but with very happy lyrics about our freedom in Christ. It doesn't fit.

I don't find instructions in the Bible about the style of music we should use. In the book of Psalms, our biblical "hymnal," a variety of feelings are expressed, including sadness (42), trust (23), and happiness (34). Some psalms were to meant to praise the Lord (8) or give thanks (103), others were for encouraging themselves while traveling (121), some provide teaching (119), and others ask for forgiveness (51). Psalm 150 calls us to use a variety of instruments, such as trumpets, harps, lyres, string instruments, flutes, and cymbals. The psalm invites us to praise the Lord "with tambourine and dance". All this suggests that a variety of styles are allowed. But we must also make the best music we can, according to our capacities and gifts, because it is for the Lord.

I know churches that have been divided over this issue. But most come to some kind of agreement. Some churches have two services, one traditional and one contemporary. Other churches mix two styles in the same worship service. My recommendation is that we all try to be a little more flexible, while seeking to worship "in spirit and in truth."

5) Planning the Worship Service

The service should be organized according to the theme of the sermon. Hymns and songs, biblical passages, and comments should reflect the same theme. The sequence in the worship service should be logical and easy to follow.

Above all, worship should explain the gospel. People should experience the gospel as they participate in the different parts of the worship service, "walking through the gospel." That is, they should recognize the attributes of God (such as His majesty, His holiness, His justice, His grace, and His love), they should acknowledge their sin, be reminded of what Jesus has done for us, receive the forgiveness of their sin, give thanks, and commit themselves again to the Lord. Participants must leave the worship "refreshed," "clean," and with a renewed relationship with the Lord.

A possible order of worship could be like the following:

- Call to worship. (Read a brief Bible passage.)
- Personal prayer of preparation. (In silence, each person prepares to be in God's presence.)
- Singing of a praise song. (Highlight some attribute of God.)
- Confession of sins. (Either each person prays in private, or a leader might pray on behalf of the congregation.)
- Promise of forgiveness. (Read a Bible passage about forgiveness.)
- Sing several worship songs. (They should be related to the topic of the sermon.)
- Time of sharing testimonies and prayer requests. (If the congregation is large, the leader might share the testimonies and needs that he is aware of. Another option is that a member of the congregation could share his or her personal testimony.)

- Pastoral prayer. (Pray according to the needs and blessings shared by the congregation, and also for the country and for the world.)
- Offering
- Sermon
- Sing a final praise song. (It should respond to the message of the sermon.)

REVIEW QUESTIONS

1. What does the Greek word translated "worship" literally mean?

2. What is the main purpose of the worship service?

3. What are the two essential factors in worship, according to John 4:24?

4. What is the "regulative principle" of worship ? How does the author understand it?

5. What are the author's suggestions about the style of music in worship?

6. What should people experience as they participate in the different parts of worship?

REFLECTION QUESTIONS

1. What are the worship services like in your church? Who plans them? What kind of order do they follow?

2. Is there anything that could improve in your worship services? Explain.

EXERCISE

Plan a worship service. First, think of a possible Bible passage or topic for a sermon. Then select the music, the Bible passages, and plan the order of service.

6.2. Prayer

Think about the following guidelines:

Read MATTHEW 6:9-13.

What can we learn from this passage about prayer?

Often our prayer times in home groups or at church focus on health needs or material needs. It is not wrong to pray for those needs, but the prayers we find in the Bible focus more on spiritual needs.

Read EPHESIANS 1:15-23.

Note the key elements of Paul's prayer in this passage.

Prayer should usually include:

- Confession of sin
- Thanksgiving for the Lord's blessings

- Praise for God's attributes
- Petitions

Prayer should be according to God's will. To pray "in the name of Jesus" doesn't mean simply to end the prayer by saying "in the name of Jesus, amen," but to ask for what is in agreement with His will, to ask for what He Himself would ask. The idea is to put yourself in Jesus' place and ask, "what would please Him?"

The best way to make sure that we are praying according to His will is to use the Bible. We should let the Word orient our prayers, recalling biblical concepts and passages. We should claim the promises in His Word. Why not keep the Bible open and use it during prayer time? Psalms are especially good for helping us to sense the presence of the Lord and to praise Him for His attributes. You may want to read passages aloud as you pray.

Prayer should be sincere. We don't have to impress anybody. We are simply talking with the Lord. We should avoid the following:

a) Repetition
b) Long prayers
c) Preaching in the form of a prayer
d) Gossip in the form of prayer
e) Clichés that are meant to sound "spiritual"
f) Using a special tone of voice that is meant to impress people with your "spirituality"

Conversational Prayer

To avoid these problems in group prayer, you could practice what is called "conversational prayer." It is a more spontaneous and natural way of praying. Instead of a few people praying once each, and for a long time, more people pray briefly, perhaps a single sentence or two, like "Thank you Lord for the beautiful day!", or "Please give me wisdom to make the right decision tomorrow." People can pray several times if they want. In other words, it is more like a conversation at the dinner table, in which everyone takes turns participating.

To learn to pray this way in a group, the first few times you may have to ask them specifically not to pray for more than a minute. Some are going to pray several times and others may not pray at all, but it doesn't matter. The idea is to make the participation more free and flowing. One of the group, probably the leader himself, should be designated to finish the period of prayer when it seems that everyone who wanted to pray has participated.

REVIEW QUESTIONS

1. What is the main focus of most of the prayers in the Bible?

2. What elements should prayer include?

EXERCISE

Have a time of group "conversational" prayer, either with your study group, or with friends or family.

6.3. Teaching

The purpose of this section is to give some general principles of Christian education, as well as some guidelines about how to prepare a Bible Study. We hope your church has Sunday School classes, both for children and for adults. Many churches also establish Christian schools. However, it's not the purpose of this book to explain how to organize a Sunday School program, or how to establish a Christian school. We mention these possible options for you to consider as part of your church's ministry. But for now, consider these general principles of Christian education:

a. The Goal

Read EPHESIANS 4:11-16.

What is the goal of teaching?

Read 2 TIMOTHY 3:16-17.

For what are the Scriptures profitable?

What is the result of teaching the Scriptures?

Some of us may fall into the pattern of just imparting information and teaching theoretical doctrines, without practical application. Others may focus on emotions, but their teaching is not based on the Bible. Finally, some teaching emphasizes practical application, but lacks a biblical basis and proper motivation.

Good teaching is balanced, without leaving any of the three aspects aside: doctrine, practice and emotions, or "head, hands, and heart."

The GOAL of Christian education is that <u>we all become like Christ</u>.

b. The Role of the Teacher

Read the following passages, and note what Jesus frequently did as He taught.

MARK 10:2-3

LUKE 7:41-42

LUKE 10:36

What do these examples teach us about the role of a good teacher?

A good teacher is an agent of learning. He knows how to ask good questions, and lets the students look for answers. A good teacher dialogues with the students, and lets them see for themselves what the Bible teaches. He helps students learn for themselves.

Frequently a teacher thinks almost exclusively about what he is saying and not about what the students are actually *learning*. If he expresses some good ideas, he thinks he is teaching well. However, it is possible that the students are not interested in the same ideas or do not understand him, or are bored. A good teacher knows how to put himself in the place of the students, identify with them, and speak their language. A good teacher gets the students to participate. It is said that a student retains very little of what he hears, more from what he experiences, and almost everything that he discovers for himself.

THE ROLE OF A TEACHER is <u>to be a learning agent.</u>

A good teacher knows how to <u>ask good questions.</u>

c. Studying a Bible Passage

A simple guideline for studying a Bible passage is the following three step process:

A. *Observation*

1) Read the passage several times, observing the details. Look for people, places, time, key words, and any other details. Read different translations.
2) Write down questions about the passage that come to your mind. For example, maybe you don't understand some word or phrase, maybe something seems to be in contradiction with another Bible teaching at first, or maybe you are curious about the historical background.

B. *Interpretation*

1) Look for answers to your questions, first in the same chapter, then the same book, then any other parallel passages. You may want to read the notes in a Study Bible or read a commentary. You may want to look something up on the Internet or in Bible study software.
2) Write down your tentative answers to the questions.

3) Write down a summary of the meaning of the passage, as you see it.

4) Reflect on how the passage fits in with the rest of the Bible.

5) Think how the passage fits in with the plan of salvation. What does it teach about Christ and the gospel?

6) Write down any other thoughts you have on the passage.

Application

1) Look for practical applications. This could be: a) a promise to claim, b) a new concept to rejoice about, c) an example to follow, d) any moral principle to follow.

2) Write down your thoughts of how to apply the passage to your spiritual life, to your family, to your work, or to any other aspect of your life.

d. A Key Tool for Teaching

Read JOHN 15:1-7.

Read JOHN 10:9.

What tool does Jesus use for teaching in these passages?

Jesus was the greatest expert in the use of good illustrations. In fact, the whole Bible is full of them. Most people learn and remember best when they can visualize something. They learn profound truths from concrete analogies.

How many times have you heard a class or sermon without any illustrations? Do you remember anything about them? Probably not! Now think of some teaching that made an impression on you, something you still remember. Did it have any good illustrations? Probably so! In fact, it would not be surprising if the only thing you remember clearly are the illustrations! What does that tell you about their importance?

For example, I remember a sermon about how Christ took our place when He died on the cross. Instead of just explaining the concept in an abstract way, the pastor talked about the story of Barabbas. He helped us imagine the scene when he was in prison waiting to be punished. Possibly he heard the crowd say his name, "Barabbas!" Then he heard, "Let him be crucified!" (Matthew 27:21-22). The crowd was shouting about Jesus, but maybe he thought they were talking about him! When they came to get him, he was probably sure he was going to die,... then they let him go free! The pastor asked us to imagine what it might have been like for him as he was walking away, probably looking back at Calvary to see Jesus on the cross. Jesus died instead of him! This teaching was very moving to me and it impressed on me the concept that Christ died for me. Of course, I think it is also good to explain the theological concept of the atonement. But the illustration was a great help for understanding and remembering this important teaching.

A KEY TOOL FOR TEACHING is the use of good illustrations.

f. Preparing a Class or Bible Study

A good teacher prepares his or her class well. It would be good to plan a series around a specific goal and theme. This could be the study of a book of the Bible, or it could be a certain topic. For example, the goal may be for everyone to learn to forgive people who have offended them. Then, each class would be oriented around that theme.

One of these classes could be based on John 13:1-15, "Following Jesus' example of forgiving."

A good class or Bible Study should include:

a. An introduction to create interest in the subject
b. The study of the Bible passage
c. Application of the Bible passage
d. An activity in which the students participate

The plan for this class or Bible Study might be something like this:

Topic: "Following Jesus' example of forgiving"

(Open with prayer)

a. Introduction

- Mention how difficult it is to forgive someone who has offended you.
- Ask if they have ever struggled to forgive somebody.
- (This is not to share their experiences yet, but only to stir interest in the topic.)
- Tell a story about an experience of your own, or of someone else, when it was hard to forgive.

b. Bible Study: John 13:1-15. Ask questions about the meaning of the passage, such as:

- How did Peter respond when Jesus started to wash his feet?
- What did Jesus say to Peter?
- Why do you think Jesus said something so strong?
- What did Jesus mean when He said that not all of them were clean?
- What does the washing symbolize?
- What attitude is expressed by washing someone's feet?
- What does this passage teach us about forgiving?
- Must the person who offended us "deserve" to be forgiven before we forgive him?
- What does it really mean to forgive?
- What does it mean for God to forgive us?
- Does He literally forget our sin? Or does He decide to not punish us for our sin?

c. Application. Ask questions such as:

- Have you ever struggled with forgiving someone? What did you do? Did you ever forgive him or her? What helped you? (Now they can share their experiences.)
- What keeps us from forgiving?
- What helps us forgive?
- What attitude should we have when someone offends us?
- Do you think an attitude of feeling superior to the person who offended us sometimes keeps us from forgiving?

- Are we really superior? (Thinking about how God sees us.)

d. Activity

Have two volunteers act out the scene of Jesus washing Peter's feet. One should sit in a chair and the other kneels down as if he were going to wash the feet of the other person. (He doesn't need to actually wash his feet.) Have them repeat the dialogue of Peter and Jesus. Ask how the person felt who was sitting in the chair. Ask the person kneeling down how he or she felt.

Talk about how this illustrates forgiving, and what we can learn from this example of Jesus. Especially, what does this teach us about the proper attitude we should have.

(Close with prayer.)

REVIEW QUESTIONS

1. What is the goal of Christian education?

2. What is the role of a teacher?

3. A good teacher knows how to _____.

4. What is one of the key tools for good teaching?

REFLECTION QUESTIONS

1. Mention some special teaching that made an impact on you and that you still remember. Why do you think you remember it?

2. In what ways can you become a good "learning agent"? How could you improve your method of teaching?

3. What has been especially significant to you in this section?

EXERCISE

Plan a class or Bible Study, taking into account the points made in this section.

Recommended Additional Reading:

1) Hendricks, Howard. *Teaching to Change Lives*. Colorado Springs: Multnomah, 1987.
2) Richards, Lawrence O., and J. Gary Bredfeldt. *Creative Bible Teaching*. Chicago: Moody Press, 1998.

6.4. The Sacraments

The sacraments are ceremonies instituted by the Lord Jesus Christ to teach the promises of the gospel with material symbols. They are visible and tangible preachings of the gospel. Protestants speak only of two sacraments, baptism and the Lord's Supper, which replace circumcision and the Passover of the Old Testament, respectively.

We say that the sacraments are *signs and seals* of His Grace because they symbolize the promises of salvation by grace (they are signs) and have the official approval of God Himself (like a king's *seal* on an official letter). God commands us to practice these sacraments and He promises to bless us in doing so.

There are differences of opinion as to who should administer the sacraments. Some think that only pastors can do it, and others think that elders can also. Since I see no difference in authority between a pastor and an elder, as explained previously, I see no biblical reason why elders should not do it. Technically, they hold the same office. However, the common practice is that pastors lead in the administration of the sacraments, while elders and deacons help.

a. Baptism

Preparation for baptism is a perfect time to go over the basic doctrines of the gospel and make sure the person being baptized is really trusting Jesus alone for his or her salvation. For those who also baptize the children of believers, it is a good time to review the gospel with the parents. The day of the baptism can also be a great opportunity to meet other family members.

The Meaning of Baptism

The Roman Catholic doctrine of baptism is that, by the very act of being baptized, the person receives forgiveness of sins, is regenerated, and receives the Holy Spirit. The *Catechism of the Catholic Church* says:[58]

> 1213 Holy Baptism is the basis of the whole Christian life, the gateway to life in the Spirit (*vitae spiritualis ianua*), and the door which gives access to the other sacraments. Through Baptism we are freed from sin and reborn as sons of God; we become members of Christ, are incorporated into the Church and made sharers in her mission: "Baptism is the sacrament of regeneration through water in the word."

> 1263 By Baptism all sins are forgiven, original sin and all personal sins, as well as all punishment for sin.

The Protestant doctrine is that the sacrament of baptism in itself does not produce spiritual regeneration or forgiveness, but that it represents the promises of salvation.

Pedro Arana, a pastor from Peru, says:

---

[58] *Catechism of the Catholic Church* <http://www.vatican.va/archive/ENG0015/_INDEX.HTM> Oct. 10, 2017.

The Presbyterian Church in Peru has to fight against two dangers that have stalked the Church of Christ throughout its history. The first is to convert the sacrament into a magical and mechanical rite. The priest Juan Luis Segundo, speaking of the Roman Catholic Church, referred to baptism as "a machine for making Christians." ... The second danger is to reduce the sacrament of baptism to a purely formal rite and a social celebration. [59]

Read ROMANS 6:3-8.

According to this passage, what does baptism symbolize?

Read COLOSSIANS 2:11-13.

According to this verse, what does baptism symbolize?

Comparing verse 11 with verse 12, this passage suggests that the New Testament sacrament of baptism is parallel to what Old Testament sacrament?

Read ACTS 2:38.

What things does baptism symbolize, according to this verse?

When Peter says "repent and be baptized...FOR the forgiveness of your sins," he is not saying that the sacrament

---

[59] Pedro Arana Quiroz, *Iniciación Cristiana* [Christian Initiation] (Lima: Ediciones Presencia Reformada, 2012), 82.

itself causes us to be forgiven, or that we should be baptized in order to be forgiven. This would contradict many other key passage in the New Testament that teach salvation by grace through faith alone (Romans 1:16-17, Romans 3:28, Ephesians 2:8-10, for example).

The word in Acts 2:38 translated "for" is "eis" in Greek, which usually means "into" or "in," and here it should be understood as "in representation of" the forgiveness of sins. The idea is that when one *repents and believes in Christ*, he is forgiven, and baptism *symbolizes* this blessing. In other words, baptism does not *produce* forgiveness. Notice that the same Greek word "eis" is used in Romans 6:4, "We were buried therefore with him by baptism *into* death,..." Obviously, this verse does not mean that baptism produces death!

We say that baptism is a visible preaching of the gospel, because it symbolizes the covenant promises: the forgiveness of our sin, our death to sin, our new life in Christ, and the reception of the Holy Spirit. Another special aspect of this sacrament is that it is done to testify publicly to a person's reception into the Christian family. When someone is baptized, it indicates that he or she has been included in God's people, with all the benefits of the covenant, just as circumcision represented this in the Old Testament. In theological terms, it symbolizes belonging to the "visible church."

Who Should Be Baptized?

There are differences among Protestants regarding who should be baptized. Unfortunately, this question continues to divide denominations. Some churches baptize only adults, after they have professed personal faith in Christ. They argue that the examples of baptisms in the New Testament are of adults who had manifested saving faith, and that baptism is evidence of new life in Christ. [60]

Other churches also baptize the children of those who profess faith in Christ, which is the Presbyterian position. Basically, they baptize the children of believers because they belong to the People of God, the covenant people, and should receive the sign which indicates so. The male children of the Jews were circumcised as a sign that that they belonged to the nation of Israel. Now, since the time of the New Testament, the sign of belonging to God's people is baptism, and it should be applied also to the children of believers, since they also belong to the "visible" Church.

This illustration might help understand the Presbyterian view: Suppose a family moves from one country to another, for example from Chile to the United States, and they become citizens of the new country. The parents would surely go through the process so that their children could also become citizens and have the documentation to show it. For Presbyterians, baptism is something like that. It does not guarantee their salvation, but indicates that they will be receiving certain blessings because of their participation in the church. Furthermore, they consider that there are two passages which, even though they do not say so explicitly, they suggest that the children of believers were baptized: Acts 16:14-15 and Acts 16:33.[61]

---

[60] Wayne Grudem, *Systematic Theology* (Leicester, England: Inter-Varsity Press, 1994), 969-970.

[61] Louis Berkhof, *Systematic Theology* (Grand Rapids: Eerdmans, 1996), 632-633

The Ceremony

There are also different views about how the ceremony of baptism should be done, whether by immersion or aspersion. I personally believe that the mode does not matter, that it can be done either by aspersion or immersion.

Those who insist on immersion as the only way usually present the argument that the Greek word for "baptize" (*baptizo*) always means to *submerge*, and conclude that the person should be put under water. But the biblical evidence shows that this is not correct.

Read LUKE 11:38.

In Greek, the word that has been translated "wash" is a form of *baptizo*.

In this context, do you think they are talking about a washing by immersion of their bodies before eating?

Furthermore, in Acts 1:5, it says that the apostles would be "baptized" by the Holy Spirit on the day of Pentecost, and in Acts 2:17-18, it says that the same event was a fulfillment of the prophecy in Joel, where he says that the Holy Spirit would be "poured out" on them.

Read ACTS 1:5 and 2:17-18.

We see from this that to "baptize" can also refer to pouring, and that baptizing could be done this way to symbolize the promise of receiving the Holy Spirit.

However, since Romans 6 indicates that baptism also represents death and resurrection with Christ, it seems appropriate to baptize also by immersion. In cases in the Bible, when they were baptized in a river, it does not expressly state that they put the person completely under water, but it is certainly possible.

At least it is clear that baptism should be done in the name of the Father, the Son and the Holy Spirit, and that water should be used to represent the gospel promise of cleansing and forgiveness.

The meaning of the sacrament should be explained to the congregation, and questions should be addressed to the person baptized, asking him to express his faith in Jesus as Lord and Savior. If you accept the view that children of believers can also be baptized, at least one of the parents should be a believer, and in this case the questions are directed to the parent or parents.

For the baptism itself, you can simply say, "_____ (name of the person), I baptize you in the name of the Father, the Son, and the Holy Spirit." Questions should also be addressed to the congregation, so that they express their commitment to pray for the person and support them in his or her spiritual life. Finally, a prayer should be made for the person baptized.

b. The Lord's Supper

The Meaning

Read MATTHEW 26:26-29.

What does the bread represent?

What does the wine represent?

Read 1 CORINTHIANS 11:23-26.

What does the Lord's Supper proclaim?

This sacrament symbolizes many things: the death of Christ for our sins, the unity of believers, our dependence on the Lord, the fact that He lives in us, and the future heavenly supper with Him. The special emphasis of this sacrament is to remember the death of Christ for us.

Catholics believe that the bread and wine really become the body and blood of Christ as they enter the mouth of the believer. Protestants believe that the bread and wine are symbols, but special symbols. They were chosen by the Lord to communicate something special. Just as the Bible contains words that are symbols especially chosen by God to reveal His Thoughts, the sacraments contain visible and tangible symbols especially chosen by God to reveal the truths of the gospel. Furthermore, we believe that the Holy Spirit is present in a special way when the sacrament is administered to believers.

Who should take part?

Read 1 CORINTHIANS 11:27-29.

What should each person do before taking part?

What should we discern?

This passage shows that the person who participates should be able to "discern" the body of Christ. He or she should understand that the Lord's Supper symbolizes the death of Christ. But Paul is also speaking here of recognizing that the believers participating are one body in Christ. In this context, they were experiencing conflicts, and Paul is insisting that the sacrament symbolizes their unity in Christ.

The participant should be a believer. Some churches recite a creed such as the Apostles' Creed before participating, saying that all who believe the doctrines cited are invited to participate. Other churches say they must be members of a church that believes in the Bible and the fundamental doctrines of the gospel, because this indicates that they have made a credible public profession of their faith. I grew up in a church that only allowed members of the same denomination to participate.

No guideline can guarantee that all participants are true believers. I certainly think that to limit participants to the same denomination is too strict. To offer the sacrament to those who belong to a certain kind of church seems like a good guideline, but it also has complications. How do we explain what kind of church they should belong to? There are many denominations that don't have a solid biblical foundation, or good theological criteria, and many people may not understand when we say they should belong to a "Bible believing church" or an "evangelical church," for example. I personally think there is room for freedom and for different approaches to "fencing the table." Clearly we should explain that it is only for Christians, and it is definitely a great opportunity to explain what it means to really believe in Christ.

As for children, they should be old enough to understand the meaning of the sacrament. Parents should talk to their children to make sure of that, and then hopefully explain this to the leaders, before their children participate. Ideally, they would have expressed their personal faith in Christ by becoming members of the church.

The Ceremony

It's good to use a biblical passage such as Matthew 26:26-29 or 1 Corinthians 11:23-34 as a guide for the ceremony. There are different ways of serving the bread and wine, depending on the number of people who are participating, the circumstances, and the physical arrangements. Probably the most common way is to have the elders pass through the congregation distributing the bread first, and have everyone wait to participate together, then distribute the wine, and again have everyone wait to participate together. Others ask the participants to form a line and walk forward to receive the elements one at a time. Some offer the same cup to everyone, while most prefer to use small individual cups. Some use real wine, while others use grape juice. Since there may be people present who have had problems with alcohol, it would be good to at least to have juice as an option. The same applies for people who can't consume sugar; it would be good to offer some option without sugar. However, there are no fixed rules for most of these matters. The main thing is to guide the people to meditate on Christ and His death for us.

Before the ceremony, it is important to talk over the details of how it will be done.

We recommend these steps as a good option for administering the Lord's Supper:

a. First, explain to the congregation the meaning of the sacrament, and explain who can participate. Remind them that it is not a sacrament for those who are perfect or for "saints", but for those who recognize that they are sinners and have accepted the sacrifice of Christ in their place.

b. Pray, asking the Lord to set the bread and wine apart for a special use, to communicate His grace to the participants, and that the Holy Spirit apply this visible preaching of the gospel to their hearts.

c. Distribute the bread. This is a good time to read portions of either Matthew 26:26-29 or 1 Corinthians 11:23-34. Invite them to eat the bread together, reminding them of what Jesus said: "Take and eat, this is my body."

d. Distribute the wine. Invite them to partake, reminding them that Jesus said, "Drink of it all of you; it is my blood of the new covenant, shed for the forgiveness of sins." Some churches listen to music while people are waiting to receive the bread and wine. Others read Bible passages, speak encouraging words, or pray.

e. At the end, confirm the meaning of the sacrament and encourage the people to know they are forgiven and have eternal life in Christ.

f. Finally, close in prayer.

REVIEW QUESTIONS

1. What are the sacraments?

2. What is the meaning of baptism?

3. What is the meaning of the Lord's Supper?

REFLECTION QUESTIONS

1. Any suggestions about how the sacraments should be administered?

2. Any doubts about some of the points mentioned in this section?

EXERCISE

Practice a ceremony of baptism and practice the administration of the Lord's Supper. Afterwards, talk about how you might do some things differently.

Chapter 7: Our Ministry Activities; Part 2

You have entered, my God,
into a long silence.
You are completely absent.
Nothing in you moves.
You are a huge cathedral without music,
the dark background of stones,
old and buried.
O Lord, what can I do when you are silent?

Hernán Montealegre
"El Silencio de Dios"
[The Silence of God][62]

Some feel that God does not listen or respond to them, that He is silent. We know it is not true, but still that's the way they feel. We are the voice that can bring the gospel to unbelievers, and we can be the Lord's hands and feet to help those in need. In this lesson, we will look at the following ministry activities: evangelism, service and fellowship.

---

[62] Leopoldo Cervantes-Ortiz, ed. *El Salmo Fugitivo; Antología de Poesía Religiosa Latinoamericana.* (Barcelona: Editorial CLIE, 2009), p. 479 (translated by the author.)

7.1. Evangelism

a. Personal Evangelism

Suppose you were the only Christian in the world. If one single person were to become a Christian because of your testimony within a year, and then each one of you led another person to the Lord in the following year, and this process continued, doubling the number of Christians each year, in how many years would everyone in the world be a Christian? Two hundred years? A hundred years? No......

...It would be only 33 years!

That's encouraging, isn't it? It means that the task of evangelizing the world is not impossible. If every Christian does his part, praying for a friend or some contact he has, seeking the opportunity to share the gospel throughout the year, we could become billions more Christians, and the world would be transformed! If each member of your church asks the Lord to convert a person during this year through his testimony, and the Lord grants that request, the church would double in a year!

Evangelism can be done through personal conversation, by loaning a person a book, inviting someone to church, organizing conferences, and many other ways. To reach new people in Chile, we taught English classes, held conferences, and had breakfast groups in hotel restaurants. Often the most effective method is to follow up on friends, family, and contacts of those who participate in your church. The way we evangelize will vary according to the person and the situation, but we can give some general guidelines.

Read 1 CORINTHIANS 15:1-4.

What are the essential points of the gospel, according to this passage?

It's good to share our testimony, it's good to talk about our church, and there are many important doctrines we can talk about. However, if we don't talk about Christ and what He has done for us, we haven't really shared the *gospel*. The gospel includes at least these two basic points: Christ died for our sins and rose from the dead.

It's also important to explain how we *receive* salvation. In theology, we speak of "redemption accomplished" and "redemption applied." Some people would agree with the facts about Jesus (redemption accomplished), but are not personally trusting Him for their salvation (redemption applied). They may be trusting their own good works, counting on the "points" they supposedly have gained by suffering, relying on the efficacy of the sacraments of the Church such as baptism and the Eucharist, or maybe a combination of these things.

I would suggest the following guidelines:

a. Get Acquainted

Evangelism should be natural, not forced. To talk about Christ should come in normal conversation. And we should be interested in people just because of who they are, not only as people to evangelize. We need to develop interest in them and learn to ask good questions to get acquainted.

b. Share Your Testimony

As the Lord provides the opportunity to share something about your own life, you can talk about your spiritual pilgrimage. Most people will listen respectfully.

c. Explain the Gospel

Here we will give one possible option for sharing the gospel. It may not be the best way for everyone. After learning this presentation, you may want to modify it or add to it, making it your own personal method. It is basically adapted for people who have some knowledge of the Bible and hold to some basic truths of Christianity, but are not trusting Jesus for their salvation yet. It would be appropriate for many people in countries that have a history of Christian influence, whether it be Protestant or Roman Catholic.

There are two questions from *Evangelism Explosion*[63] that are very helpful, because they reveal whether a person is trusting in Jesus. They are like this:

1) If you died today, do you think you would go to heaven?
2) If you died and went before God and He asked you, "Why should I let you into heaven?", how would you answer Him?

Often people answer that they are not sure they would go to heaven. Some people think it would be arrogant to be sure. In that case, you can explain that it is possible to be

---

[63] James Kennedy, *Evangelism Explosion* (Chicago: Tyndale House Publishers, 1977).

sure, and that it is not arrogant, because our salvation depends on Jesus, not on us. We are all sinners, but Jesus came to die on the cross in our place, to pay the penalty for our sin. He rose from the dead in victory over death and sin, and He promises to save all who believe in Him. It's a matter of believing what God Himself has promised.

The second question of *Evangelism Explosion* is even more revealing. Many people say they have tried to be good, that they were not as bad as other people, or that they have not done anything terrible, like killing someone. We want to help the person understand that we are all sinners, and that salvation is a gift of God, by grace, not something that we earn by our own merits.

We can focus on Romans 3:23, John 3:16, and Ephesians 2:8-9.

If you quote Bible verses, it is good to use a modern translation. In fact, it might be better to paraphrase the verses or sum up the main point in your own words.

"For all have sinned and fall short of the glory of God." (Romans 3:23)

"For God so loved the world, that he gave his only Son, that whoever believes in him should not perish but have eternal life." (John 3:16)

"For by grace you have been saved through faith. And this is not your own doing; it is the gift of God, not a result of works, so that no one may boast." (Ephesians 2:8-9)

Next it would be good to use some illustrations. For example, the movie "The Mission" lends itself very well to explain the difference between gaining salvation by merits and receiving it by grace.

In "The Mission," a Spaniard named Mendoza has been selling indigenous slaves in South America during the time of the Spanish colonization. A priest makes him do penance for his sin by climbing a steep cliff, near where the tribe lives, pulling a sack of heavy objects by a rope. When he can go no further, he looks up and sees people climbing down toward him, with knives in their hands. He recognizes that they are from the same tribe where he was capturing slaves, and is sure that they are coming to kill him. But to his surprise, they cut the rope, and the huge sack falls tumbling down the cliff. He is free! Mendoza understands from this that they have forgiven him, and he breaks down crying.

This scene shows two perspectives. The penance required by the priest represents human effort to earn forgiveness, and the cutting of the rope by the indigenous is like God's free forgiveness by grace. We are all sinners, incapable of satisfying God's demand for righteousness. Just like Mendoza could not climb the cliff, we can't earn our salvation. But Jesus earns it for us by living a perfect life in our place, dying on the cross in our place to pay the penalty for our sins, and by rising again from the dead to gain the victory. In a sense, He "cuts the rope" to forgive us and set us free.

Salvation depends totally on the grace of God. It is a *gift*. The only thing we need to do is believe sincerely in Christ. Good works are the *result* of our salvation, not the *cause* of it.

Now we want to live a life pleasing to Jesus, not to earn our salvation, but simply because we love Him. And the strength to live a changed life comes from Him, not from us.

We are like light bulbs. A light bulb itself does not produce light; it is only an instrument. The electricity is the power that produces the light. In our spiritual lives, God is the electricity, and we are His instruments, connected to Him by faith in Christ. Our changed lives are the light produced by the work of the Holy Spirit in us.

A third illustration is from a video about a man who fell in a hole.[64]

A man falls into a deep hole and can't get out. People pass by offering suggestions. One recommends that he meditate until becoming conscious that the hole does not really exist. Another suggests doing something to accumulate good "Karma," in order to be reincarnated as something good. Then someone says that he should do spiritual exercises. The man tries all these things, but remains in the hole, and eventually collapses, tired of all the efforts. Finally, another man stops and looks down, throws a rope into the hole, climbs down, puts the man on his shoulders, and carries him out.

The first people who give suggestions represent other religions. The man who goes down to carry him out represents Jesus, who came to earth to save us. We are

---

[64] "A Man in a Hole" YouTube:
<http://youtu.be/OEpoHO_Ox6A> (August 1, 2013)

totally incapable of getting ourselves out of the hole of sin and guilt, but He puts us on His shoulder and sets us free!

The most important thing to remember about evangelism is to let the Holy Spirit guide you. Be open to adjust the conversation according to the person's response, and be sensitive to the way the Holy Spirit is directing things.

REVIEW QUESTIONS

1. What are the essential elements of the gospel?

2. What two things should we do before sharing the gospel?

3. Summarize the presentation of the gospel suggested in this section, including:
    a. the two introductory questions
    b. the three Bible passages, and
    c. the three illustrations.

4. What is the most important thing to remember about evangelism?

REFLECTION QUESTIONS

1. Do you have any suggestions about personal evangelism?

2. What have been some of your best experiences of sharing the gospel?

3. What have been some of your difficult experiences in trying to share the gospel?

EXERCISE

Ask two people to practice presenting the gospel. Ask one to represent a non Christian and the other to play the role of a Christian. Afterwards, talk about the positive aspects of the presentation and about how it could be improved.

Other Recommended Resources

For studying in small groups, or with an individual, you might try *Am I Good Enough?* It's a Bible Study manual that explains the basic doctrines of salvation in a simple way.

Ramsay, Richard B. *Am I Good Enough?*
Lawrenceville, GA: Christian Education and Publications, 2008.

b. Planting a New Church

Lord willing, a church that is healthy and growing will eventually plant a daughter church. The most convenient way is to form a group of people from the mother church that are willing to cooperate in the new project, and who live in the area where you want to start the new church.

This book is not a church planting manual, but here we would like to offer just a few practical suggestions:

1) Prayer

Planting a new church is a wonderful ministry, but it is complex and can be difficult. Therefore, it calls for much prayer. Only the Lord can give growth (1 Corinthians 3:6), so all activities should be covered with prayer.

2) Planning

Decide on the location of the new church.

Ideally, it would be an area where there is no other evangelical church. Hopefully, it would be where the group of initial participants live, because they will already have contacts there. If not, it should at least be easily accessible for them.

Do a demographic study.

It would be helpful to do an analysis of the sector. Find information such as: average age, percentage of men or women, location of schools, location of other churches (if there are any, including Catholic churches), location of commercial centers, average income, average level of education, and common occupations. Often this kind of information can be found in the Internet, in census reports, or in municipal offices. This will help you plan how to reach the people of the sector.

Take a survey.

You can also learn a lot about the needs of the community by doing a survey. You may ask one simple question, like "What are the greatest needs of this community?" Or you might ask, "How could our church best help this community?" You could go to a commercial center or some public place and ask at least 20-30 people at random. You may need permission to do this some places.

Afterwards, analyze the answers. Note two or three of the greatest needs of the area.

This information will help as you consider what kinds of ministries you will emphasize. If family conflict is a serious problem, you could offer conferences about family. If there is a problem of poverty or drug addiction, you could consider how to help these needy people.

Read JEREMIAH 29:7.

What should we seek for the city where we live?

What blessing do we receive in return?

(Note: The word translated "peace" or "welfare" is "shalom" in Hebrew, which means a complete kind of well-being.)

Select the leaders.

An important step in the process of planting a church is the selection of leaders, because the church will become like its leaders in its character. Make sure they fit the qualifications that we studied previously.

Draft the vision, the mission, and the motto

Follow the guidelines given previously in chapters 2 and 3 to write a vision statement, a mission statement, and a motto.

3) Training Leaders

This very book would serve as a training manual for the leaders.

4) Evangelism

There are many options:

Friends and Family

The best contacts are the friends and family of those who are participating the church plant. Encourage them to invite them to social activities, meals, birthdays, and such. Encourage them to seek the opportunity to share their faith. You could use the suggestions in the previous section to help them learn to share the gospel.

Evangelistic Activities

In order to meet new people, you might consider activities such as the following:

- Breakfasts for men in a restaurant
- Teas or breakfasts for ladies
- Marriage conferences
- Conferences on other topics of interest
- Concerts
- Classes of some kind, maybe languages, maybe computer skills, for example

In our last church planting project in Chile, we made our first contacts by teaching English classes. We did not directly evangelize during the classes, but we got acquainted with new people.

We discovered that many men in our area of the city were not comfortable attending a Protestant church service. But they were willing to go to an informal breakfast at a restaurant. We would have an unstructured time of just enjoying breakfast and chatting, then we would have an open discussion about some topic of common interest, or maybe talk about a movie or a book that was popular at the time. The subject was not necessarily a "spiritual" subject, but we could always bring up some connection with Christianity.

One man was a high official in the navy. For him, it was difficult to attend an evangelical church, but he hardly ever missed the men's breakfasts. Once he said that the breakfasts were his "church."

The women did something similar with their teas. The neutral place and the informality are important. So is our attitude. My wife, Angelica, insists that we should avoid building "walls" between us and new people. Unintentionally, we tend to communicate that we do not consider them Christians. Without knowing for sure, we just assume it. This produces a barrier between "us" and "them." Angelica talks to new people as if they were Christians. That is, she talks freely with them for example about her relationship with God, or about something she has learned from the Bible, assuming they will be able to identify with her. If they are not Christians, they are not offended, and in fact it helps them realize that they are missing something really wonderful.

Small Home Groups

In our experience, small home groups are the most effective way to reach new people and also to disciple new Christians. These meetings can be prayer meetings, Bible Studies, or fellowship groups. See the suggestions for small group meetings in another section below.

5) Starting Public Worship Services

It is better to wait until you have at least 20-30 people participating to have a public worship service. Otherwise, it can be rather discouraging. Also, if a new person comes and sees only 10 people there, it will seem strange. While the group is still small, you can continue meeting in homes.

When you begin public services, you need to adapt some things for new people. The service should be serious, but also joyful. New people should sense an atmosphere of acceptance and friendliness. They should never be made to feel embarrassed about being new. For example, instead of simply telling people to look up a Bible passage, like Jeremiah chapter 3, help them locate it in the Bible by giving them the page number, or by telling them it is about half way through the Bible, or something like that. It might be even better to project the reading on a screen so that all can read it. The same applies to the music. In other words, try to avoid anything that would make new people feel uncomfortable or out of place.

In the beginning, one of the most serious problems is finding a place to meet. Some options are: a school gymnasium, a hotel conference room, an office space, an empty store space at a shopping center, or the church building of another denomination (you can meet later in the day).

Your greatest enemy can often be discouragement. Remember that God only asks you to be faithful, not to produce results. Only He can give growth. Leave that to Him!

Remember 1 Corinthians 3:6: "I planted, Apollos watered, but God gave the growth."

REVIEW QUESTIONS

1. Note the steps of church planting mentioned in this section:

1) P_____

2) P_____

    Decide on the L_____ of the new church.
    Do a D_____ S_____.
    Take a S_____.
    Select the L_____.
    Draft the V_____, the M_____, and the
       M_____.

3) T_____ the L_____

4) E_____

5) Starting the P_____ W_____ S_____

REFLECTION QUESTIONS

1. What things can impede church planting? How can you avoid them?

2. What are some of the most difficult aspects of planting a new church?

3. Do you feel called to plant a new church? How and when might you do it?

EXERCISE

Draw up tentative plans for planting a new church.

7.2. Service

a. General Introduction

Although the deacons are especially responsible for helping with the physical and material needs of people, they also deal with spiritual matters. The meaning of their office and a list of their characteristics and common duties are described in a previous chapter.

It is complicated to know the best way to help needy people. When I first went to Chile, I was concerned about inequality. I wanted to bring lots of money from the United States so that Chileans could have a similar standard of living. But after a few years, I began to realize that this was not exactly the solution.

I had also been reading books about injustice and oppression, but began to understand that the causes of poverty were complicated and multiple, not only injustice. Furthermore, I was learning to take into account other important factors such as self-sufficiency and independence. As the saying goes, "Give a man a fish and you will give him food for a day, teach him to fish and you will feed him for the rest of his life." For example, if a town has no drinking water, it would be better to help them find the way to have their own source of water, instead of taking them water every day. Where there are many diseases, it would be better to help eliminate the causes of those diseases, and not only treat the sick.

One of the best examples of an integral ministry I have seen is an Independent Baptist mission in Haiti. They have a church, a hospital, an institute, and workshops where they teach people to do be electricians, mechanics, and carpenters. They have a restaurant on the side of the road, and even a zoo for visitors. They also grow little pine trees to give away. This is important in Haiti, because they have cut down many trees for firewood, and this has caused them to lose good soil on the mountain sides. The missionaries take the little pine trees and show people how to plant them in a way that allows them to restore the land. Their integral ministry is a good example of how to create independence and self-sufficiency.

Dignity should also be preserved as we help the needy. If we do it the wrong way, we may damage their self-esteem. To understand this, think of the following example: Suppose that a man works five years to save up enough money to buy a used car, a little old, but he likes it. Since he has worked so hard for it, he really appreciates it. He cleans it and takes care of it because it means a lot to him. Now suppose a rich foreigner comes to visit and offers to give him a brand new Mercedes Benz. It would be difficult to refuse, right? But how will he feel about the five years he worked to buy his old car? What does this do to his self-esteem and dignity? Would it really be worth it? Some things are more important than having nicer material possessions. (Also, will he be able to pay for the maintenance of such an expensive car?)

For some time, I thought it would be difficult to be happy with few material possessions. But over the years, I have come to see that many poor people are happier than many rich people. I will never forget a visit we made to a poor family in Chile that lived in a small wooden shack. After doing a Bible Study with them, Angelica and I asked them what they would like us to pray for. I asked, "Is there something you need?" I looked around the house thinking, "They don't have a refrigerator, they only have one bed for them and the baby, and they have hardly any other furniture. If I were in their situation, I would have a long list of prayer requests!" But they answered, "No, we can't think of anything!" I wanted to cry. But on the other hand, I was glad to know that they were able to be content with the few things they had. I can't help but compare them with some fairly wealthy people I know that seem less happy. Some complain a lot and seem to be tangled up in taking care of their house and cars and many other possessions.

Nevertheless, people need sufficient food, clothes, and a secure place to live. It is almost impossible to be happy without those things. It is also important to have enough to pay bills, without being strangled by debts. Many families in Latin America, Africa and Asia struggle to meet these essential needs. I have seen little cardboard "houses" in the trash dumps. I have talked with people that can't pay their light bill or water bill. I have faced a young man who didn't have even enough small change to take a local bus to a hospital where his father was dying. I am also aware that many people live where oppressive governments and unjust economic systems keep them from rising above their misery. I still would like to minimize the enormous gap between the very rich and the very poor. I just want to say that, before simply giving things away, maybe just in order to feel better about ourselves, we need to think carefully about the best way to help people.

I see three key principles in the Bible about managing financial things: honesty, diligence, and compassion. Any plan we have to help the needy should reflect those three principles.

Read PROVERBS 6:6-11.

Does this passage highlight the principle of honesty, diligence, or compassion?

Read PROVERBS 11:1.

Does this passage highlight the principle of honesty, diligence, or compassion?

Read PROVERBS 21:13.

Does this passage highlight the principle of honesty, diligence, or compassion?

Read LEVITICUS 25:13-17.

Was it permissible for a person to work diligently to improve his situation and buy the land of another person? Or was complete equality of land ownership required?

What was to happen to the land during the Year of Jubilee? How would this affect the distribution of property and wealth over the generations?

It would not be good to help the needy in a way that destroys their own initiative, or that damages their sense of dignity, or that develops a situation of continued dependence. But sometimes it is necessary to modify unjust situations that keep producing poverty and suffering. And we should always show compassion.

Jesus had compassion on the needy. We can't separate the two arms of ministry extended to the world: evangelism and service.

Read JOHN 13:1-5.

What did Jesus want the disciples to learn?

Read MATTHEW 25:31-36.

Note the ways in which we can serve our neighbor that are mentioned in this passage.

Read MATTHEW 25:40.

When we help a brother, who are we helping?

Read GALATIANS 6:10.

Whom should we help first?

Read JEREMIAH 29:7.

What does this tell us about serving the community near our local church?

Norberto Quesada writes: [65]

> The Church as a faith community also expresses its missionary character in acts of love. Juan Drive says that the Church is a community that "communicates to the world the reconciling love of God." [66] The same idea is corroborated by Washington Padilla, when he says that "the mission of the Church is to serve..."[67]

REVIEW QUESTIONS

1. What factors should be considered when we plan how to help the needy? What aspects are more important than material possessions?

2. What are the three key principles regarding finances in the Bible?

3. Mention some ways in which we should help the needy, according to the New Testament.

---

[65] Norberto Quesada, Tesis doctoral, capítulo 1.

[66] Juan Driver, *Comunidad y compromiso* (Buenos Aires: Certeza, 1974), p. 76.

[67] Washington Padilla, *Hacia una transformación integral* (Buenos Aires: F.T.L. 1989), p. 15.

REFLECTION QUESTIONS

1. In what ways does your church help the needy? What other ways could you help them?

2. How can we avoid taking away the dignity or independence of the needy as we help them? Give examples.

EXERCISE

Take a survey of your church members, and another of your neighborhood to see what the greatest needs are.

Then develop a project to help meet the needs of your church and your community. For example, if the needs are related to family conflicts, hold conferences on marriage and family. Maybe you can set up a counseling center. If there are problems with drug and alcohol abuse, maybe you can open a rehabilitation center.

b. "First Aid" Counseling

Counseling is a compassion ministry, helping people with family conflicts, emotional problems, spiritual problems, or other types of problems. Many leaders don't feel qualified to do counseling, because they think it is something only professionals can do. Certainly it is good to recognize our limitations, and sometimes we should recommend that the person seek help from someone with more experience or someone who has been better trained in this field. Furthermore, it would be a great blessing for our churches if more leaders sought special training in this area and opened counseling centers.

However, even if you do not have special training, you still can do some counseling. Every Christian, since he has the Holy Spirit and the guidelines of Scripture, can help a lot simply by listening, praying, and sharing biblical teachings.

> And let us consider how to stir up one another to love and good works, not neglecting to meet together, as is the habit of some, but encouraging one another, and all the more as you see the Day drawing near. (Hebrews 10:24-25)

Some people us the term "first aid counseling" for this type of counseling. Notice that, according to verse 24 of Hebrews 10, one aspect of counseling is to help each other to love more and to live more consistently according to God's Word. Notice also another aspect of counseling in verse 25, to "encourage." The word translated "encouraging" comes from the verb *parakaléo* in Greek, which comes from two Greek words, "para" (beside, next to) and "kaléo" (call). In verses like John 14:16, a form of this word is used to refer to the Holy Spirit as the "Comforter" (paraklétos). This illustrates another aspect of the counselor's ministry: to come alongside the person and give encouragement and comfort.

My friend Richard Crane has a lot of experience in counseling. He says that there are two abilities that we need to develop in order to be good counselors: learn to ask good questions, and learn to listen.

The questions should be open, not so simple that they can answer just "yes" or "no." For example, instead of asking,

"Did that make you feel sad?", it would be better to ask, "How did that make you feel?"

The questions should also help find deeper problems underneath the more superficial problems that the person might be talking about. It is good to look for details about their situation, and also about the background. For example, if a married couple is having conflicts, you might ask each one to tell his or her version of how the problem started and how it has developed. Ask them to give concrete examples of what is happening.

In order to listen well, it might help to repeat what you think the person said, but in other words. For example, you might say, "I understand you are saying that your husband is not paying attention when you talk to him, is that right?" Don't put ideas into the person's head, going beyond what he or she said. For example, if a woman is saying that her husband is not paying attention when she talks, it would not be helpful to say, "So you think your husband doesn't love you, right?"

Let the person explain himself or herself. The simple act of expressing themselves can help a lot. It's also important to avoid quick and simplistic answers. Don't just quote a Bible verse and think that you have done a good job of counseling. In the case of a conflict between two people or more, don't give the impression that you have taken sides.

Try to help the person find his own solution, without pressuring him to do something before he himself is convinced. Once I pressured a young lady to make a decision, thinking that it would be best for her. She finally agreed. But soon after, I learned that she had changed her mind and didn't really follow through with it. She wasn't really convinced.

Of course, in the appropriate moment, after listening and guiding the person to seek his own solution, it would be good to offer biblical guidelines and prayer. But we need to learn to be patient, guiding, but not pressuring or hurrying.

All problems come from the Fall and its results. However, the consequences of sin are complex. We suffer because of our own sin, we suffer because of the sins of others, and we suffer because of the effects of sin in creation and in our own physical bodies. Furthermore, these factors are all interrelated. It is not always easy to identify exactly how these factors are causing the problem we are encountering.

Even so, in counseling we can help the person reflect on their own responsibility and also on their way of responding to other people who have hurt them. If the counselee is guilty of something, he should repent, ask for forgiveness, and change his attitude and behavior. If other people have offended him or her, they may have to talk to the them, and they need to forgive them ((Matthew 18:15-35).

We should leave the person with hope. It will help to remind him that the Lord directs everything for our good, including our difficult experiences (Romans 8:28, James 1:2-4). It will give comfort to reflect on the promises that the Lord loves us, understands our struggles, and will provide a way to resist trials and temptations.

> For we do not have a high priest who is unable to sympathize with our weaknesses, but one who in every respect has been tempted as we are, yet without sin. Let us then with confidence draw near to the throne of grace, that we may receive mercy and find grace to help in time of need. (Hebrews 4:15-16)

No temptation has overtaken you that is not common to man. God is faithful, and he will not let you be tempted beyond your ability, but with the temptation he will also provide the way of escape, that you may be able to endure it. (1 Corinthians 10:13)

All counseling should be based on the gospel, on grace. We should not make the counselee see his sin without pointing to forgiveness in Christ (1 John 1:8-9). We should not encourage him to change his attitude and behavior, without reminding him that only Christ can help him change (Galatians 2:20, 2 Corinthians 12:9-10). Finally, we should not assume that the person is really a Christian. A counseling session can be an excellent opportunity to bring a person to faith in Christ.

Another practical suggestion is to avoid counseling a person of the opposite sex alone. I have heard of men counselors and ministers that have fallen into temptation when they were alone with a woman. I also know of ministers who have done nothing wrong, but have had to leave the ministry because a woman accused them of something inappropriate. If there is no other witness present, it will be your word against the other person's.

REVIEW QUESTIONS

1. What is "first aid counseling"?

2. What are the two most important abilities that a leader should develop in order to be a good counselor?

3. Mention some ways we can help people who seek counseling, according to Hebrews 10:24-25, Romans 8:28, Hebrews 4:15-16, and 1 Corinthians 10:13.

REFLECTION QUESTIONS

1. Have you had a good experience in giving "first aid counseling" or in receiving it? Explain how it helped the other person or how it helped you.

2. Do you have other suggestions for being a good counselor?

EXERCISE

Practice a conversation of "first aid counseling." One person should play the role of a church member with a problem, and the other person plays the role of a church leader who tries to help. Afterwards, talk about what was done well and what could be done better.

Recommended Additional Reading:

1) Gary Collins, *Christian Counseling; A Comprehensive Guide*, Nashville, Tennessee: Thomas Nelson, 2006.

2) Jay Adams, *Competent to Counsel*, Grand Rapids: Zondervan, 1986.

3) Larry Crabb, *Effective Biblical Counseling: A Model for Helping Caring Christians Become Capable Counselors.* Grand Rapids: Zondervan, 1977.

4) Norman H. Wright, *Crisis Counseling; What to Do and Say in the First 72 Hours. A Practical Guide for Pastors, Counselors, and Friends.* Ventura, CA: Regal Books, 1993.

5) Paul David Tripp, *Instruments in the Redeemer's Hands*, Phillipsburg, N.J.: P&R Publishing, 2002.

c. Administration

Man is made in the image of God, and one important aspect of that image is the ability to administer things. God governs the entire universe, organizing and carrying out His plan. When man administers things well, it reflects something of God's nature.

Read GENESIS 1:28.

What task did God give man?

We are administrators, or stewards, of the whole world. Pastors tend to dedicate their time to preaching, teaching, and other activities, but not much time to administration. However, the church needs good administration, and if the pastor can't do it, they should get help. One of my seminary professors said, "If you become a pastor and have to choose between calling a co-pastor and hiring an administrative secretary, hire a secretary!" Many churches may not be able to hire an administrator, but every church needs people who can help in this area.

1) Planning

A church shouldn't just let things happen spontaneously. Near the end of the year, the leaders should meet to make plans for the following year. Or maybe you prefer to plan quarterly. What are the goals? How can we try to reach them? The plans should be communicated to the congregation in order to create an atmosphere of expectation, and to get everyone involved. Ideally, you could make a calendar of activities. And you definitely need a financial budget!

2) Evaluation

Planning doesn't help much if there is no evaluation. I would recommend that the leaders meet once a month to pray and to evaluate how things are going.

Normally the elders would evaluate the spiritual aspects of the church, and deacons would evaluate the financial and material aspects. The elders would analyze things like attendance, membership, teaching, small groups, leaders, and any problems that have occurred. The deacons would evaluate things like the budget, the giving, the maintenance of the property, and physical needs of the sick and elderly.

To evaluate properly, there should be some methods for obtaining information. For example, there should be a list of members, a record of attendance, a report on meetings and activities, and periodic surveys to get feedback on the worship service, the teaching, preaching, and other activities.

3) Managing Finances

We can't stress enough how important it is to manage finances correctly. It requires people that you can trust completely, and who have the gifts for it. You need several people involved. Unfortunately, I have seen too many cases where somebody has given in to the temptation to "borrow" money from the church, then can't pay it back. At least three people should count the offering together, and three people should be required to sign checks and to prepare the financial reports. The financial situation should be reviewed regularly, hopefully monthly.

4) Discovering Gifts and Knowing How to Delegate

Good administration includes knowing how to identify the gifts of others and how to delegate responsibilities. Every member has some gift and some role to play. When a member feels he has nothing to contribute, he may lose interest and seek another church where he can use his gifts.

Read 1 CORINTHIANS 12:12-27.

What is the main point of this passage?

Is there any insignificant gift in the church body?

Is there any member that has nothing to contribute?

REVIEW QUESTIONS

1. Why is administration important?

2. What are the four aspects of administration mentioned in this section?

1) P_____

2) E_____

3) M_____ F_____

4) Discovering G_____ and knowing how to
    D_____

REFLECTION QUESTIONS

1. How does administration function in your church? Do you have a special administrator? How do you make plans? How do you evaluate them?

2. How could you improve administration in your church?

3. How are finances managed in your church? How could you improve this?

4. Do you think your members are using their gifts? How could you help them use them better?

7.3. Fellowship

a. General Introduction

People are very lonely today. During a period of time in the United States, most people wanted to move to the suburbs, looking for more space and more privacy. Now the tendency is to return to "walkable" urban centers where they are closer to other people. The popularity of social networks such as "Facebook" indicates the strong desire to connect. "Cheers" was a popular show about a tavern that promoted itself by saying it was a place "where everyone knows your name."

The longing to have friends and to relate to other people is part of the image of God in man. God himself is a God of fellowship, a God of three persons who had fellowship among themselves from all eternity. When God created the first man, he said that it was not good for him to be alone, and therefore He made the first woman. But the Fall has affected all relationships between people, and has caused an empty sense of loneliness in the hearts of people.

Salvation is the restoration of all relationships, first between man and God, but also between man and his neighbor, man within himself, and man with creation. Salvation takes place in the context of a community. The people of God began as the family of Abraham. Then the nation of Israel was formed under the leadership of Moses. Now the people of God is the community of believers all over the world, the Church.

The local church should be a center of fellowship, a Christian family. Unfortunately, sometimes churches do not seem like a family, especially when they are large.

In Chile, we participated in the founding of several new churches. Since there were few people in these new congregations, we experienced a close sense of family. Every Sunday in worship, before the pastoral prayer, we would ask if anyone had a testimony or any special requests. It was a very special time of sharing. When we had the Lord's Supper, we would form a circle, and then hold hands to sing. Of course we wanted the congregation to grow, but we enjoyed the close ties to people in our small church.

When we were in the early stages of planting one of these churches in Chile, we made a trip to spend a year in the United States. Our son Nicolas was born while we were there, and the next Sunday I went to church, where there were over 500 in attendance. I will never forget how I felt sitting in the pew that day. I wanted to stop the service and scream that Nicolas had been born! Thankfully, I didn't need to shout, because they mentioned it in the announcements. But this experience made me realize that there are certain benefits in small churches. There are advantages of a large church too, but we shouldn't look down on small congregations. And if a church is large, it's very important to form small home groups.

Years later, we participated in another large church. This church had small home groups, and I taught the Bible study in one of them. We had come to know the members of the group, and we had shared both joyous experiences and difficult tragedies. It was like a family. I remember what happened when the father of one of the members of our group died. Her father lived in another country, and the congregation didn't know him. The following Sunday, I remember watching as this woman came into church and walked up to sit in one of the front pews. The pastor didn't know that her father had died, and during the time of announcements, they didn't say anything about her father. After the service, I noticed that she was walking out with her head down, and I thought to myself, "how terrible that no one knows what she is going through." But in that moment, I saw a couple from our group go give her a hug and express their condolences. We later did the same. Thank the Lord for that home group!

Read ACTS 2:43-47.

How did they express their fellowship?

What can we learn from this example?

Read ACTS 4:32-37.

How did they express their fellowship?

What can we learn from this example?

There are many ways to share. Personally, I think small groups in homes are the best way to practice fellowship. In another section, we'll talk more about these groups.

The church where we are attend now in Miami has many small groups that gather during the week to eat, share, pray, and study the Bible. Every once in a while, the men of the group get together early for coffee and talk, before they go to work. Our church has a meal on Wednesdays for all members, and offers a Bible study afterwards. Some members play sports together. Special dates like Christmas always provide an opportunity to celebrate together.

Furthermore, we have special meetings and activities for young people, for ladies, and for seniors.

Many churches offer coffee and light refreshments before or after worship. That allows people to stand around and talk for a while. Our church has sofas, tables and chairs in the entrance of the church, where people can sit and talk. We can learn a lot from successful cafes that provide a comfortable and relaxed atmosphere. Why not do something similar in our churches?

REVIEW QUESTIONS

1. Why is fellowship so important?

2. Explain how fellowship reflects an aspect of our salvation.

3. How was fellowship expressed in the churches of the New Testament, according to passages like Acts 2:43-47 and Acts 4:32-37?

REFLECTION QUESTIONS

1. What things does your church do to provide fellowship?

2. What could your church do to provide even more fellowship?

b. Home Groups

Small groups should include Bible study and prayer, but do not necessarily require the presence of a pastor or elder. The general supervision of the groups, and the training of their leaders, is the responsibility of the elders and pastors, but they are not the only ones who can lead a group. Practical suggestions for teaching and leading prayer can be found in the previous chapter of the book.

As mentioned above, small groups have always been important to our family. We established them in the churches we planted in Chile, and they were always key centers to evangelize, to share, and to grow. They were the essential platform for developing the spiritual life of our churches. As mentioned above, we currently participate in a group that has become like a family for us.

In the early church, meetings took place mainly in homes. The evangelistic force was no longer "centripetal", inward, but "centrifugal", outward. As mentioned before in another chapter, in one sense, the Lord began to prepare His people for this outward movement during the period of captivity in the Old Testament. At that time they couldn't go to the temple in Jerusalem, so they established synagogues in every area of the Mediterranean. Thus the movement no longer focused on one central place.

Jesus commanded the disciples to go make disciples of all nations, of all ethnic groups. Paul fulfilled the Great Commission to go outward, traveling to many places around the Mediterranean. Instead of building a large cathedral for all the new Christians, they established meetings in homes. They didn't begin to build large cathedrals until the fourth century.

Read ROMANS 16:3-5.

What was being held in the house of Prisca and Aquila?

Read PHILEMON 1:2.

What church did Paul greet in this verse?

In the last decades, there has been an extraordinary growth of the evangelical churches in Cuba and in China. In both countries, this growth occurs especially in small groups. In Cuba, until recently the government did not allow churches to buy land and construct new buildings. Therefore, most churches formed small groups in houses to evangelize and disciple people. I know of a local church that at one point had 500 small groups. I heard of a pastor who had an evangelistic service in which fifteen people were converted. The pastor began to teach them the fundamentals of the faith, having classes with them, every day from Monday to Friday of the first week. By Friday of that first week, every one of the fifteen new believers had formed a new group in their own home!

Norberto Quesada, president of the Evangelical denomination in Cuba, *Los Pinos Nuevos,* says:

> If we start with the fact that the church is not necessarily a place, but a congregation or gathering of the saints, then houses can be (and indeed have been) propitious places for the manifestation of the *ekklesía* of Christ.
>
> ...
>
> Home meetings always bear fruit because they are constantly growing. Churches that have changed their concept of church have solved the problem of space and costs that a new church plant requires. Home meetings allow the members and ministry to be taken outside of

our four walls to the place where it is most needed and where Jesus sent us (Matthew 10:16).[68]

Suggestions

1. The Schedule

I recommend weekly meetings or bi-weekly meetings.

I suggest beginning with light refreshments, then a time to share, and finally a Bible Study. In our group, we try to take 30 minutes for refreshments, 30 minutes for sharing, and 30 minutes for the Bible Study. We are not strict about the timing, but our group likes to have an idea about how long the meeting will be. In other countries and other cultures, this can vary greatly. Each group will need to adapt to the people and the cultural expectations.

Refreshments should be light and easy to prepare, so that it doesn't become a burden, and so that it doesn't become a culinary competition. This relaxed time is also great for interpersonal sharing.

The group sharing time should be informal and relaxed. It is not easy for everyone to share personal things, and nobody should be pressured. It should be sufficient to ask simple questions like "Has anything special happened this week?" or "Does anybody have something to share, or something to pray for?" As you meet regularly over time, you will know how to follow up on certain things. Maybe somebody had an operation, and you can ask how things went. Maybe another family took a trip, and you can ask what they enjoyed most.

---

[68] Doctoral Thesis for *MINTS International Seminary.*

It's important not to ask embarrassing questions, or ask anyone to share something that might be very personal or private.

2. Group Dynamics

a) Don't pressure anybody to talk, to read, or to pray. Some people feel uncomfortable, and may even feel panic when asked to do these things in a group. The leader can encourage people to share, and he can help develop an atmosphere of acceptation, but he should not force anyone to do something.

b) Don't criticize anyone when they share, and don't give simplistic advice. It is not a therapy session, and people often don't need your advice; they just need to share. If they want your counsel, they will probably ask for it.

c) You don't need to correct every error. If something really serious has been stated that could be confusing, maybe something heretical, you need to say something. But if you do, first make sure you really understood the person correctly. Also, be careful to speak gently and kindly, expressing positive feedback as well.

d) Remind the group that personal things shared in the group must remain private among the group.

e) Try to avoid letting one person dominate the discussion. You might need to say something like, "Thank you, (name). What do the others think?" or "I'd like to hear everybody's opinions." Look the others in the eye, and avoid looking too much at the person who tends to dominate.

3. The Bible Study

Many guidelines have been given in the previous chapter on teaching, but we will repeat a few suggestions specifically for home groups:

a) Normally, it is good to study through a book of the Bible, taking a passage at a time, or selecting key passages. You might also use a study manual on a book of the Bible or a topic of common interest.

b) The key to a good Bible study is to ask good questions. The best questions are the questions that you yourself have. Look for your own answers before the study, but let the others share their own thoughts and opinions during the study, before sharing yours.

c) It's good to ask questions in the three categories of observation, interpretation, and application.

d) It's always important to give illustrations, especially stories about true life situations.

4. Outside the Meetings

The group should hopefully become like a family. The men or women can get together for coffee or lunch once in a while. Our group also has dinners together on special occasions. When people are struggling with a problem, such as a sickness, not only the leader, but also others from the group, should call them on the phone and maybe go visit them. We just went through a crisis of a hurricane, and everyone kept in touch to see how each other was doing, offering help if necessary. It was very encouraging!

REVIEW QUESTIONS

1. In the early church, where did they usually meet?

2. What are some of the advantages of home groups?

3. What kind of schedule is recommended for a home meeting?

4. What are the suggestions for managing group dynamics?

5. What is the key to leading a good home Bible Study?

REFLECTION QUESTIONS

1. Does your church have small home groups? How do they work?

2. Share your experiences, both positive and negative, from home groups.

EXERCISE

Make plans for a home group meeting.

Make a list of questions for a home Bible Study on some passage. Don't forget to include observation, interpretation, and application questions.

c. Pastoral Visitation

This ministry has been lost in many churches, but still has an important place in the church. It should be a normal part of the work of the pastor and the elders especially, but also the deacons. It enables the leaders to do what they are called to do, to watch over the spiritual life of the members.

It is best to arrange a visit beforehand, and not arrive unannounced. The visitor should not go alone, but with another person. If you are visiting a woman or women without men present at the home, at least one of the visitors should be a woman.

The purpose is to show interest in the family, evaluate their needs, and minister to them with the Scriptures and prayer. The visit should be brief and friendly.

I recommend the following guidelines for a first visit to church members or to people who have visited the church:

a. Carry on lighter conversation at first, so that everyone can relax. Ask typical questions such as how long they have lived in the area, where they came from originally, what kind of work they are involved in, if they have children, and so on. Ask questions that show interest in them, but without asking anything too intimate.

b. Afterwards, ask about their participation in the church. How long have they been attending? How has their experience been in the church? How could the church serve them better?

c. If you sense that they would be comfortable with such questions, ask them about their faith. If they are church members, we assume they are Christians. Ask them to share their testimony about how they became Christians.

d. If for some reason, you think they may not be Christians, the dialogue should change to evangelism. See the previous chapter for suggestions about evangelism.

e. Ask if they have any prayer requests.

f. Read a brief Bible passage and pray for them.

For future visits, you can focus on their continuing needs. As time goes on, they should become more comfortable with your visits and possibly share more personal needs. Always read a passage and pray for them. Let them know that you are always available if they need to talk about anything.

Pastoral visitation becomes even more important for the sick, for those in the hospital, and for the elderly. They need to be encouraged. However, normally it's not good to spend more than a few minutes with the sick, to avoid making them tired.

I have two friends who are great examples of pastoral visitation: Don Wheatley and Bill Cox. Don was a school teacher for 30 years. During one year, he became sick and was hospitalized eight times. This led him to retire from teaching and dedicate his time to visiting others in the hospitals of Baltimore. He usually reads a Bible passage and prays with the patients, and is always prepared to share the gospel when he gets the opportunity. He has discovered that more people are willing to talk about eternal life and their relationship with God than we would have expected. Sometimes sick people are thinking a lot about death, and really want to talk about spiritual things, but others around them are afraid to talk about it. Don is very friendly, and always encourages the patients. Nurses often look for him and ask him to talk to patients that are discouraged.

Don has written a book of testimonies about his visits, and added some suggestions about visitation.[69] Here is a summary of some of the points he mentions for hospital visitation:

---

[69] Donald Wheatley, *Adventures in Mercy*. Published personally.

a) It is important to get permission to visit if the person is not from your own church.

b) It would be good to wear some kind of identification.

c) Prepare beforehand with prayer.

d) You need to find out the following information about the patient:

- Who is he? Where is he from?
- Who is with the patient? Some family members?
- What happened? What is his physical situation?
- How can you help?
- What is his spiritual situation?

e) It is good to read some Bible passage, something positive about God, then also pray, showing hope and faith.

f) You might take some cards with appropriate Bible verses, then ask if they would like for you to leave one of them.

g) You might also offer to leave a New Testament, hopefully one that also has the Psalms.

Bill Cox is a staunch defender of the need for elders to do pastoral visitation. He himself has learned by visiting along with Don Wheatley. He has been an elder most of his life, and considers that visitation should be an essential part of an elder's work. He recommends dividing the members of the congregation, and organizing the elders so that every member is visited on a regular basis, at least once a year. He suggests keeping records of each visit, noting things that you observe, so that the pastor can know about any issue that needs more attention.

REVIEW QUESTIONS

1. What is the purpose of pastoral visitation?

2. Mention the recommended guidelines for a first visit to a church member or to someone who has visited the church:

a.
b.
c.
d.
e.
f.

3. Note the suggestions of Don Wheatley for hospital visitation:

a.
b.
c.
d.
e.
f.
g.

REFLECTION QUESTIONS

1. Do you have any other suggestions for pastoral visitation? Anything for hospital visitation?

2. Have you ever had someone make a pastoral visit to you? Was it a good experience? Explain how it went.

3. Have you ever made a pastoral visit to someone else? How did it go?

EXERCISE

Make a pastoral visit with a pastor or elder who has some experience doing it. Talk afterwards about what you learned from it. What are some positive things? What things could be done better?

Chapter 8: Our World; Challenges and Opportunities

"The times, they are a changin'."
Bob Dylan, 1964

"Things have changed."
Bob Dylan, 2000

The whole Bible is an eloquent testimony
of God's intention to meet and dialogue with man
in his concrete historical situation.[70]
René Padilla
Argentina

8.1. Socio-cultural Factors

More than 500 years since the Reformation, we live in a very special time. Things are changing quickly, and our churches will have to adapt to the new generations in order to communicate the gospel in an effective way, and in order to minister to the current needs. The gospel message itself is the same, but we may need to express it differently and defend it differently. We need to know the social, cultural, philosophical and religious factors that characterize our world today, not only to face the challenges they present, but also to take advantage of the opportunities they offer.

---

[70] René Padilla, *El Evangelio Hoy* [The Gospel Today] (Buenos Aires: Ediciones Certeza, 1975), 56.

a. Technological Advances

I have heard Dr. Richard L. Pratt, Jr. compare our situation today with the time of the Reformation. He says that they had a single new invention, the printing press, which allowed them to saturate Europe with good literature, but now we have many new inventions: television, the Internet, videos, DVDs, cell phones, and other technological advances. He insists that we should use all these means to saturate the world with the Word of God. Like most changes, new technological advances can cause problems, but we can also use them to extend the kingdom of God.

Some problems are obvious, such as the temptations that result from easy access to inappropriate sites and images. It also means that people are accustomed to being entertained, and to being able to change the channel or change the song at any time. It is sometimes difficult for a pastor to compete with TV programs and other means of entertainment.

We need to be prepared to answer the question, "Why should I go to church?" For a time, a young man who did not attend church services on Sundays visited me every week to talk and pray. I tried to encourage him to go to church, saying that he needed to hear the Word, to pray, and to participate in worship. He answered that he prayed with me, received the Word talking with me, and praised God alone in his house. I had to think of something better to say. I finally decided to remind him that he could not practice the commandment to love the other members of the Body of Christ if he never spent time with them. I also tried to explain that it should be enough to know that it pleases the Lord when we come together as a family to praise Him and receive His Word. As a parent, I can understand that there is something special about having family members together. I enjoy receiving text messages from my children, but it is much better to see them sitting at the table with the family and to talk with them in person.

Ironically, the new devices that have been designed to improve communication, can become obstacles to personal face-to-face communication. During 2015, the average number of emails sent and received worldwide was more than 205 billion per day. An individual working in an office would normally receive 88 messages a day and send 34 each day.[71] According to one source, adolescents in the United States spend an average of six and a half hours a day looking at some kind of electronic screen.[72] How many times do we see a group of people sitting at the same table in a restaurant, while many of them are looking at their cell phone or typing a text message, instead of talking to people sitting right beside them? According to another study, the greater use of screen activities among teens, as opposed to more person-to-person activities, is making them more unhappy.[73]

It is not only young people who have this problem. After a church meeting one day, I approached two men to offer my help with something, and I noticed that both of them were reading messages on their cell phone. I said, "Sorry, I'll wait until you're done." One looked at me momentarily and said,

[71] The Radicati Group, Inc., "Email Statistics Report, 2015-2019" Oct. 21, 2016. <http://www.radicati.com/wp-content/uploads/2015/02/Email-Statistics-Report-2015-2019-Executive-Summary.pdf>

[72] "Teens spend a 'mind-boggling' 9 hours a day using media" Oct. 21, 2016. <http://www.cnn.com/2015/11/03/health/teens-tweens-media-screen-use-report/>

[73] Jean M. Twenge. "Has the Smartphone Destroyed a Generation?", The Atlantic September, 2017: 59-65.

"Don't worry, we're listening," and turned his attention back to his device. I told them what I wanted to say, but it was obvious that neither of them was really paying attention. I decided I would never do that again.

There are other effects of our new technology that are not so obvious. Some authors point out how the Internet and social media like *Facebook* make it easy to promote false ideas and distorted information. The truth becomes what the multitudes seem to accept as valid. Internet search engines lead a person to become more and more enclosed in a certain world view, without the person even realizing it. As you look for information or opinions, search engines such as *Google* or *Bing* register the searches in order to identify your interests. Unless you have your program set to delete your history, the next time you look for something similar, the first links you see will be from sources of the same mindset. For example, an atheist who assumes that the Bible is full of errors and contradictions may begin looking for articles about the Bible. He will probably tend to read first the articles that show supposed errors. As he continues to investigate the subject over the next few weeks, the first options he sees will be more and more articles that support his view, and articles with an opposing view will be pushed several pages back. The reader becomes more and more convinced that hardly any intelligent person believes that the Bible does not contain errors. In fact, when this same person investigates another topic such as evolution, the search engines also point him first to links that would normally coincide with his view of the Bible. On and on it goes, building thicker and thicker walls around his worldview, making it less and less likely that he will find articles that challenge him to reconsider his views.[74]

However, new technology also provides opportunities. We live in a very special time, when we can reach remote corners of the world with the gospel. We can use the new means of communication to teach the Word of God. 3.5 billion people now have access to the Internet, over 40% of the world's population.[75] Many sites offer biblical and theological resources, such as *Thirdmill*, which has students all over the world. There are multitudes of Christian videos available, and Bible study programs like *Logos* and *e-Sword*.

In a country like Cuba, or in other countries where there is little access to the Internet, there are alternatives ways to watch videos or read materials, such as laptop computers, DVDs, "flash drives" ("USB stick"), and tablets. There is also a mini-computer called a "Raspberry Pi" which is the size of a small matchbox. By putting a small memory card and connecting an antenna, it works like a virtual Wi-fi. Students can connect their laptops and use resources that are normally accessed only on the Internet, such as the *Thirdmill* programmed courses. Students sit in the classroom, work on their laptops, and take automatically graded tests, as if they were connected to the Internet.

Some consider cell phones the most important apparatus at the moment. I understand that for many Christians in China, it is the best option to gain access to resources for

---

[74] Kurt Andersen. "How America Lost Its Mind," The Atlantic September, 2017: 76-91. Note that the author calls himself an atheist and gives examples that tend to be anti-Christian, but I find his points about how the Internet influences our thinking, and how society has become disconnected from the truth, very convincing.

[75] <https://www.statista.com/statistics/273018/number-of-internet-users-worldwide/> Oct. 21, 2016.

study. In summary, we should redeem the technological advances and use them for the extension of the Kingdom of God.

b. Church Growth

The evangelical churches are growing worldwide at an amazing rate. According to Bruce Milne, between 1960 and 2000, evangelicals grew three times faster than the world population. [76] Much of the growth has been in Africa, China, and Latin America.

At the beginning of the 20th century, almost all of Latin America was Catholic, and according to conservative statistics, now at least 11% are evangelicals (from 700,000 in 1900 to 91 million in 2010).[77] According to *Christianity Today*, in 2014 the percentage of Protestants for some countries was as follows: 9% in Mexico, 13% in Colombia, 17% in Peru, 15% in Argentina, 17% in Chile, and 26% in Brazil.[78] Evangelicals in countries like Cuba and the

---

[76] Bruce Milne, *Know the Truth: A Handbook of Christian Belief* (Downers Grove, Ill: InterVarsity Press, 2010), 332. Quoted in Wikipedia, "Evangelicalism" August 26, 2015.

[77] Jason Mandryk, ed., *Operation World*, seventh edition (Colorado Springs: GMI, 2010), 47.

[78] *Christianity Today*, "Gleanings", "Sorry, Pope Francis: Protestants Are Converting Catholics Across Latin America," Nov. 13, 2014. <http://www.christianitytoday.com/gleanings/2014/november/sorry-pope-francis-protestants-catholics-latin-america-pew.html> Oct. 24, 2016 (Results of research from *Pew Research Center*.)

Dominican Republic have doubled in the last 15-20 years.[79] In some countries such as Guatemala and Nicaragua, evangelicals have grown to as much as 40% of the population. [80]

It is an unusual blessing to live in a time of such growth. But this also presents us with some challenges, especially the need to train leaders. According to *Operation World*, in Latin America, the majority of the churches have pastors who have no formal theological training, and training for lay leaders is even less common.[81] *Thirdmill* estimates that worldwide there are at least two million pastors without biblical and theological education.[82]

c. International Migration

Many people are moving from one country to another. We live in Miami, where thousands of foreigners arrive every year, looking for a better life for their family. Many Peruvians are moving to Chile, while many Africans and Latin Americans are moving to Europe. Since the year 2000, Spain has received six million immigrants from many different countries.[83] At the moment of this writing, there are millions

---

[79] *Operation World*, p. 293 (in Cuba, it doubled between the years 1995 and 2010), and p. 309 (in the Dominican Republic, between 1990 and 2010).

[80] *Operation World*, 46. According to Wikipedia, "Christianity by Country" Nov. 11, 2014, 40% of the population of Guatemala and Honduras are non-Catholic Christians.

[81] *Operation World*, 52

[82] *Thirdmill*, <http://thirdmill.org/mission/mission.asp>, August 26, 2015.

[83] Wikipedia, "Immigration to Europe." Sept. 21, 2015. <https://en.wikipedia.org/wiki/Immigration_to_Europe>

of refugees from Syria around the world, fleeing from war. 4.5 million are in the five neighboring countries of Turkey, Lebanon, Jordan, Iraq and Egypt alone.[84]

Although many times the movement of people is the result of tragedies and difficulties, the Lord will surely use it for the extension of His kingdom. We don't need to go overseas to share our faith with foreigners. Also, often a person who has left his roots is more open to change. Muslims that would be difficult to evangelize in their own countries become more reachable when they move to a country that allows greater religious freedom.

Sometimes the evangelistic situation is turned around. That is, some immigrants are Christians, and they take their testimony to their new country. In Spain, according to *Operation World*, only 1% of the population identify themselves as evangelical Christians.[85] But many evangelicals have recently moved there from Latin America. Could it be that the Lord has sent them to evangelize the Spanish and the Muslims there?

d. Movement to the Cities

Another change that affects the ministry of the Church is the movement toward the cities. According to one study,

---

[84] Amnesty International, " Syria's refugee crisis in numbers," May 31, 2017.
<https://www.amnesty.org/latest/news/2016/02/syrias-refugee-crisis-in-numbers/>
[85] *Operation World*,
<http://www.operationworld.org/country/spai/owtext.html> May 31, 2017.

Through most of history, the human population has lived a rural lifestyle, dependent on agriculture and hunting for survival. In 1800, only 3 percent of the world's population lived in urban areas. By 1900, almost 14 percent were urbanites.... In 1950, 30 percent of the world's population resided in urban centers.

The world has experienced unprecedented urban growth in recent decades. In 2008, for the first time, the world's population was evenly split between urban and rural areas. ...It is expected that 70 percent of the world population will be urban by 2050, and that most urban growth will occur in less developed countries.[86]

This change also helps us reach new people with the gospel. Those who move to a new place, even within the same country, are more open to new friendships and new influences. Our churches can become substitute families for them.[87]

REVIEW QUESTIONS

1. What are the factors that characterize our world today mentioned in this section of the chapter?

---

[86] "Human Population; Urbanization," Population Reference Bureau. May 31, 2017. <http://www.prb.org/Publications/Lesson-Plans/HumanPopulation/Urbanization.aspx>

[87] Rodolfo Blank, *Teología y Misión en América Latina* [Theology and Mission in Latin America], (St. Louis, Missouri: Concordia Publishing House, 1996), 129.

2. In what ways are these changes both challenges and opportunities?

3. According to Bruce Milne, between 1960 and 2000, how did the growth of evangelicals in the world compare to the growth of the population?

REFLECTION QUESTIONS

1. How are the changes mentioned in this lesson manifested in your own country?

2. Do the changes mentioned in this section encourage you or worry you? Explain.

e. The Changes in Thinking and Religion

Antonio Cruz challenges us to understand current thinking, in order to communicate the gospel in our day:

> The divine mandate to take the gospel to the whole world requires a dialogue between the Christian faith and the culture of every epoch. To communicate the message of Jesus Christ adequately, it is necessary to understand the periodic changes that our society undergoes, and reflect about the latest manifestations. We need to know how the men and women think today, in order to share the Good News with them.[88]

---

[88] Antonio Cruz, *Postmodernidad* (Barcelona: CLIE, 1996), 52. Translated by the author.

Alan Hirsch suggests that in the West, we are experiencing a pluralism of thought similar to the period of the first few centuries, between the New Testament time and Constantine. With Constantine, Christianity became an accepted religion, and soon Christian culture, beliefs, and morality were a dominant influence in society. However, the spiritual power of the original grassroots Jesus movement was lost during this time. Then even the social and cultural dominance of Christianity came to an end with modern secularization, when reason and science took priority over faith. Now we again live in a situation with a wide variety of philosophies and religions. Society has become secular, and the Church has been marginalized. He argues that, while society has changed greatly, the Church has not sufficiently adapted its ways of trying to reach people with the gospel.[89]

TWO PERIODS OF PLURALISM

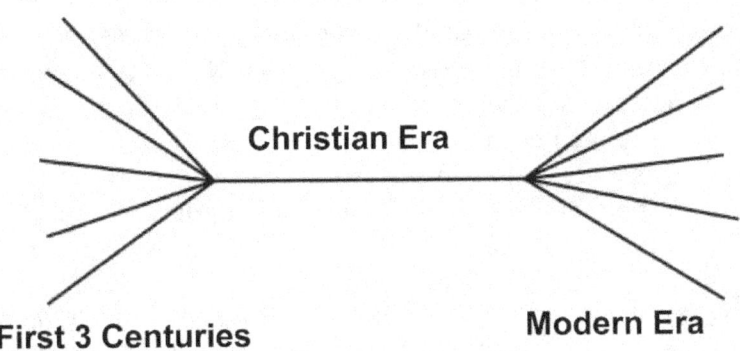

Christian Era

First 3 Centuries   **Modern Era**

---

[89] Alan Hirsch, *The Forgotten Ways* (Grand Rapids: Brazos Press, Baker Publishing Co., 2006), 58-61.

The term "postmodern" has been used in recent years to describe a new way of thinking. It is not so much a new religion or philosophy as it is a new attitude. It involves a loss of trust in science, and an increased skepticism regarding absolute truths and ethical norms. It is an eclectic and pluralistic mentality, in which everything should be accepted.

Antonio Cruz says:

> A postmodern individual...has become a vagabond of ideas. He or she does not usually hold anything sincerely. He has no absolute certainties. He is not surprised by anything, and therefore, nothing keeps him awake at night. He might change his opinion just as easily as he changes his shirt.[90]

There is also a growing interest in oriental religions and beliefs like the *New Age*, which combines western science with oriental religion. The New Age has its roots in ancient Gnosticism, which held that material things were bad, and spiritual things were good. For them, salvation came through mystical knowledge ("gnosis" in Greek). New Age followers do not reject other religions, but see them as part of a process of human awakening.

It is very common today for people to reject any expression of exclusivity. A key moral principle today is *tolerance*. When we say that Jesus is the only way, they see this as intolerant and closed-minded. They often say something like, "I believe that God is love, and I cannot believe that He would condemn someone for having another religion."

---

[90] Antonio Cruz, *Postmodernidad* (Barcelona: CLIE, 1996), 52.

We must hold tightly to our Christian truths and moral principles. However, this does not mean we can hate the people who disagree with us. The Lord has commanded us to love all people, even our enemies.

f. Persistent Problems

There are other persistent problems that should be mentioned briefly, such as poverty, education, drug and alcohol abuse, and domestic violence. While they are not new developments, we need to remember them as we consider the ministry of the Church.

a) Poverty and Hunger

The UN estimates that there are 795 million people living in hunger worldwide. In sub-Saharan Africa, the highest poverty level of any region in the world, one out of four persons is hungry or undernourished,[91] and 41% live in extreme poverty.[92] Latin America and the Caribbean have made great progress in the last 20-25 years, but in 2014, Latin America still had 28% of their population living in poverty.[93]

---

[91] Hunger Notes, "Africa Hunger Facts" June 1, 2017. <http://www.worldhunger.org/africa-hunger-poverty-facts/>

[92] UNDP in Africa, "About Sub-Saharan Africa," June 1, 2017. <http://www.africa.undp.org/content/rba/en/home/regioninfo.html>

[93] Comisión Económica para América Latina y el Caribe (CEPAL), Panorama Social de América Latina, 2015, (LC/G.2691-P), Santiago, Oct. 31, 2016. <http://repositorio.cepal.org/bitstream/handle/11362/39965/4/S1600175_es.pdf>

2) Education

During the last two centuries, there has been an enormous expansion of education and a great increase in literacy rates. However, there are still areas of serious need, such as sub-Saharan Africa, where literacy rates are still only 50% among the youth.[94] In general, there is a big difference between the level of education among the poor and among the wealthy. In Latin America, while overall, 80% of young people between 20 and 24 years of age had finished high school in 2013, only 34% of the poorest 20% of the population had finished.[95]

3) Drug and Alcohol Abuse

In the United States, binge drinking is a very serious problem (defined as 5 or more drinks within two hours for men, and 4 or more for women). One report states that one in six U.S. adults does binge drinking about four times a month, consuming about eight drinks per binge.[96] The tragedy of the young man from the fraternity at *Penn State University* highlights this problem among young people. At a party, he was forced to drink until he could hardly walk, and when he fell down the stairs and hurt himself, they refused

---

[94] Our World in Data, "Global Rise in Education," June 1, 2017. <https://ourworldindata.org/global-rise-of-education>

[95] "Panorama Social de América Latina", 29.

[96] Center for Disease Control and Prevention, Alcohol and Public Health, "Binge Drinking," June 1, 2017. <https://www.cdc.gov/alcohol/fact-sheets/binge-drinking.htm>

to seek medical help for him for 12 hours, when it was already too late to save his life.[97]

According to the *National Institute on Drug Abuse,* in 2013, 9.4 percent of the population had used an illicit drug in the previous month. This is an increase from 8.3 percent in 2002.[98]

4) Domestic Violence

Domestic violence is a growing concern. According to a report of the United Nations, 35 percent of the women in the world have experienced physical and/or sexual violence by an intimate partner, or sexual violence by a non-partner at some point in their lives.[99]

g. Uncertainty

Paul Johnson suggests that the key term to describe the 20th century was "uncertainty." The political, economic, and military instability in the world, the lack of moral absolutes, the supposed relativity of truth, and religious plurality

---

[97] USA Today College, June 1, 2017.
<http://college.usatoday.com/2017/05/05/criminal-charges-announced-fraternity-hazing-death-student-penn-state-student/>
[98] NIH, National Institute on Drug Abuse, "National Trends," June 1, 2017.
<https://www.drugabuse.gov/publications/drugfacts/nationwide-trends>
[99] "Violence Against Women," United Nations, 2015. (June 1, 2017)
<http://unstats.un.org/unsd/gender/downloads/Ch6_VaW_info.pdf>

produce a feeling of disorientation and insecurity. Nietzsche expressed this sentiment more than a century ago:[100]

> Are we not continually falling? And backwards, sideways, forwards, in all directions? Is there still an up and a down? Aren't we straying as though through an infinite nothing? Isn't empty space breathing at us? Hasn't it got colder? Isn't night and more night coming again and again?[101]

One of the famous phrases of Charlie Brown from the *Peanuts* comic strip was, "My anxieties have anxieties." Shortly before he died, in one of his last comic strips, Charles Schulz verbalized this uncertainty in the person of Snoopy. Holding tightly to his doghouse, he says,

> I find myself worrying about everything ... Take the Earth, for instance.... Here we all are clinging helplessly to this globe that is hurtling through space... What if the wings fall off?[102]

Although at first it might give the impression that these tendencies make the evangelistic task more difficult, I believe it is not necessarily so. Uncertainty often causes people to search for meaning and spiritual truth. A report from *Gordon Conwell Seminary* says that in the year 1970, only 82% of the population of the world considered themselves "religious,"

---

[100] Paul Johnson, *Tiempos modernos* (Buenos Aires: Javier Vergara Editor, 1988), 59.

[101] Friedrich Nietzsche, *The Gay Science* (Cambridge: Cambridge University Press, 2001), 119–20.

[102] Sarah Boxer, "The Exemplary Narcissism of Snoopy," *The Atlantic*, November, 2015, 108-123.

and by the year 2010, the number had increased to 88%. They project that it will be up to 90% by the year 2020.[103]

In this context, we can offer the certainty of the gospel. Hebrews 11:1 says that faith is "the certainty of things hoped for, the conviction of things not seen." The Word of God is the absolute truth (2 Timothy 3:16-17, John 17:17), and our Lord promises to work all things for our good (Romans 8:28). "If God is for us, who can be against us?" (Romans 8:31).

The world is a very needy place! There are many other important factors that we need to understand today, but we have mentioned just a few to stimulate reflection. Each church should analyze the situation of its own country, its city, and its neighborhood. What are the most serious problems? (Divided families? Poverty? Drug or alcohol abuse? Lack of education? ... something else?) What are the factors that you should take into account to have an effective ministry in your neighborhood?

REVIEW QUESTIONS

1. What are the factors that characterize our world today mentioned in this section of the chapter?

2. In what ways are these changes both challenges and opportunities?

3. Mention the changes in thought and religion during the last century.

---

[103] "Christianity in its Global Context, 1970-2020," Center for the Study of Global Christianity, Gordon Conwell Seminary, Nov. 11, 2014. <http://wwwgordonconwell.com/netcommunity/CSGCResources/ChristianityinitsGlobalContext.pdf>

4. How can these changes in thought and religion become opportunities for sharing the gospel?

5. What are the four "persistent" problems in the world, as described in this section?

6. What term does Paul Johnson use to describe the 20th century? What has caused this feeling?

REFLECTION QUESTIONS

1. What do you think about the socio-cultural factors mentioned in this section? What do they mean for our evangelistic task? How should we adapt to them?

2. Can you think of other important factors that describe our world today?

EXERCISE

Make a brief survey to research people's thinking in the neighborhood of your church. It may include some simple questions, such as whether they believe in God, in the Bible, or in life after death. Ask what they think about the church today in general, and other similar questions. It's better to have multiple choice answers.

Use the survey with a variety of people, of different ages, male and female, of different levels of education.

Draw up some conclusions about the people in your community. Then note what this means for the ministry of your church.

8.2. Contextualization

In order to reach people in our communities, we need to "contextualize" our way of teaching and our way of ministering. The truth doesn't change, but we may need to change the way we explain it. Think of the truth as nutritious peanuts. In the United States, we have M&Ms with peanuts, chocolate, and a colorful coating of sugar. But in Chile, they offer candied peanuts in the streets that have been simply stirred into cooked sugar. In Cuba and Spain they like "turrón", peanuts packed into a dense sweet chunk made from milk and honey. The peanuts are the same, but each culture packages them in a different way.

In fact, we need to "contextualize" ourselves personally, without adopting sinful ways of thinking and living, of course. Jesus Christ is our best example of contextualization, who inserted Himself into our world to save us, but was without sin.

Read ACTS 17:1-3 and ACTS 17:16-34.

What is the difference in the way Paul preaches in these two cases?

Why did he do it differently?

In what sense is Paul "contextualizing" his ministry?

Read ACTS 19:8-10 and ACTS 11:27-30.

What is the difference in Paul's ministry in these two situations?

What does this teach us about "contextualizing our ministry?

Read MATTHEW 5:1-2 and MATTHEW 8:1-3.

What is the difference in Jesus' ministry in these two situations?

What does this teach us about "contextualizing our ministry?

Read PHILIPPIANS 2:1-8.

What does the example of Jesus teach us about contextualization?

Are we reaching the new generation? Representatives of "emerging" churches think not. While I am not comfortable with some things that the emerging churches are saying and doing, I think they are making some valid points.

Eddi Gibbs and Ryan Bolger say the Church has not adapted to social changes, and that it is losing its influence. They say that during the Reformation, the Church adapted to the new culture of the printing press, but the Church today is far behind changes in society. They insist that the new generation is losing interest in churches with traditional services, because they do not offer an experience that is very different from passively watching a TV program, with little participation.[104]

---

[104] Eddi Gibbs and Ryan K. Bolger, *Emerging Churches* (Grand Rapids: Baker, 2005), 15-46.

One of their most important challenges is that our churches need to become "centrifugal" again, ministering outward, as in the New Testament times. They argue that we have a "come to us" attitude, instead of "going" to make disciples of the nations.[105]

Norberto Quesada, president of the growing "Los Pinos Nuevos" denomination in Cuba says:

> It is not conceivable, from a biblical point of view, to have a church that does not project itself toward other cultures. The Church calls the world and the nations to repentance, announcing the forgiveness of sins and a new relationship with God, through the sacrifice of Jesus Christ.
>
> ...
>
> The challenge of the contemporary Church lies in the cross-cultural extension of the gospel. God has given specific responsibilities and commandments for the accomplishment of that task. The ministries of the Church have provided the expansion of the gospel that is capable of transforming the culture where it is preached.[106]

REVIEW QUESTIONS

1. What is "contextualization"?

2. What is the concern of the "emerging churches"?

---

[105] Gibbs and Bolger, *Emerging Churches,* 50.
[106] Doctoral thesis for *MINTS International Seminary.*

3. What is the important feature of the church of the first centuries that has been lost, according to Alan Hirsch?

REFLECTION QUESTIONS

1. What do you think of contextualization? Is it valid? What are the dangers?

2. Considering the world around you, how could your church better contextualize its teaching and ministry?

3. What do you think of the comments of the emerging churches? Are they valid?

4. Reflect on Jeremiah 29:7: "But seek the welfare ["shalom"] of the city where I have sent you into exile, and pray to the LORD on its behalf, for in its welfare you will find your welfare." What would this mean for the ministry of your local church?

EXERCISE

Make a list of important factors in the sector of your local church.
For example, consider the following factors:

-Age (Are there more young people or more adults?)
-Level of education (What is the level of the majority?)
-Gender (Are there more men or more women?)
-Economic situation (How would you describe it? What is the level of the majority?)
-Greatest needs (poverty, family conflicts, alcoholism, drugs? Other?)

Write down any other important factors about the community around your church.

Recommended Additional Reading:

Hirsch, Alan, *The Forgotten Ways*. Grand Rapids: Brazos Press, Baker Publishing Co., 2006.

Johnson, Paul. *Modern Times.* New York: Harper Collins, 1991.

Myers, Kenneth A., *All God's Children and Blue Suede Shoes.* Wheaton, Illinois: Crossway Books, 1989.

Romanowski, William D. *Eyes Wide Open; Looking for God in Popular Culture*. Grand Rapids: Brazos Press, 2001.

Conclusion

I would like to encourage you to be faithful and responsible leaders. Faithful, but without feeling the impossible weight upon your shoulders to make the Church grow in your own strength. Responsible, but without feeling that the sanctification of the Church depends only on you. Don't forget that we plant and water, but the Lord gives the growth.

I would like to encourage you to always keep the bigger picture in mind, that we are building a cathedral, that we are building the Kingdom of God. You are not alone, and your contribution is a significant part of the most important project in the world!

Compare the following pictures.[107]

---

[107] This work of art is called "Wish", and is in Belfast, Ireland, done by Jorge Rodriguez-Gerada (Cuban-American). It takes up 4 hectares. <http://www.belfastfestival.com/News/WISH/> (11/11/14)

What do you think the man is doing in this picture?

Now look at the second picture. This picture is of the same thing, but viewed from an airplane. Notice the buildings and the cars that look so small from this view.

Now what do you think? What was that man doing?

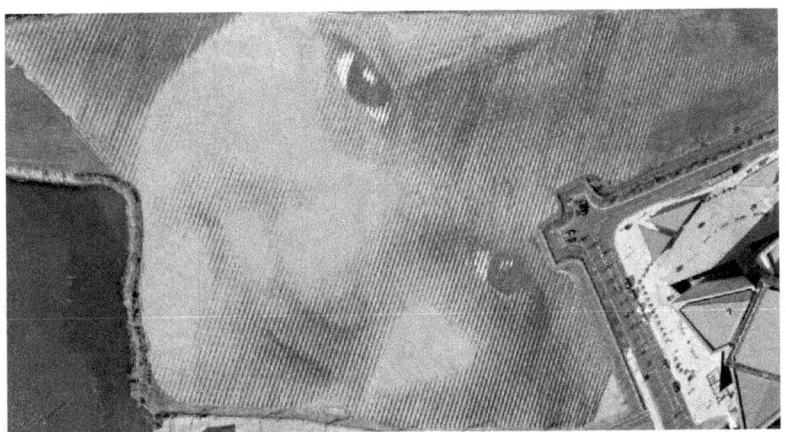

This is how it is in the ministry. Sometimes we only see what is close to us, and it seems like we are only moving sand and dirt. But our ministry is part of something much bigger, the Kingdom of God!

www.ingramcontent.com/pod-product-compliance
Lightning Source LLC
Chambersburg PA
CBHW071631140626
46555CB00022B/2058